DEBRANDING GOD

DEBRANDING GOD

Revealing His True Essence

EDUARDO STEIN

Lederer Books
A division of
Messianic Jewish Publishers
Clarksville, MD 21029

16 15 14 13 4 3 2 1

ISBN-13: 978-1-936716-70-8
ISBN-10: 1-936716-70-4

Library of Congress Control Number: 2013947624

Lederer Books
A division of
Messianic Jewish Publishers
6120 Day Long Lane
Clarksville, Maryland 21029

Distributed by Messianic Jewish Publishers and Resources
Order line: (800) 410-7367
lederer@messianicjewish.net
www.messianicjewish.net

Printed in the United States of America

DEDICATION

I honor God, when I honor them:

Eliane my beloved wife—thank you!

Ludwig Goulart my dear friend—thank you!

You both made my life easier!

Contents

FOREWORD

From the very beginning of this book, we are captured by comments on contemporary life. We then find references to art and science interwoven over several chapters that provide a beginning window into the nature of reality. Human foibles are unmasked. As we continue to read there is a transition where more and more of the wisdom of the Word of God is expressed. We find ourselves drawn into the wisdom and the answers to the human dilemma provided by Scripture. Contemporary culture, modern cultural history since the enlightenment, science, and entertainment are all somehow intertwined to unmask human existence in our own day.

As the reader continues on the journey provided by this book, he is drawn into the answers to the ultimate questions of life, death, courage, and meaning. The perspective is Messianic Jewish, but the writing is not narrow. It is universal in meaning, but especially relevant to Western cultures, including South American.

Hopefully, many readers who are immersed into the ocean of contemporary culture, are adrift, and can see no safe harbor, will be delivered from that drift and will come to the lasting city, the New Jerusalem, and the ultimate fulfillment of human life.

Daniel Juster, Th. D. First President, Union of Messianic Jewish Congregations, Director, Tikkun Ministries.

Preface

Every book is based on the assumption that each author presents him or herself or is presented by someone else.

Talking about myself is a biased task, since it would mean claiming that I am original, innovative, and creative, which is obviously only partially true.

Nobody produces entirely exclusive content—all of us are the product of some collaborative content that generated the "I." We are "I" and we are "us." We are "one" and we are simultaneously "six billion." Our individuality is our distinction, while at the same time the original and unique piece that is missing in this enormous puzzle.

Interestingly, we live in a time in which there is a lot of talk about the cloud. Not the cloud that announces God's presence in the tabernacle in the desert cited in the Torah, but the digital cloud that instead of making drops of rain, makes drops of bytes fall. Actually, the perception of the "iCloud" is that everything revolves around the "I"—Apple uses the lowercase "I" in front of some of their products, which indicated that what you're using is an extension of yourself. The cloud serves as a metaphor for the transmission of information and digital storage as a facilitator of the life of "I."

At the same time, this "metaphorical cloud" serves as the data backup and flow. With the cloud loaded with binary information, you synchronize on your devices that which is yours and that which is not yours. The ownership of ideas becomes a common property with ethical restrictions for those who are ethical. There is a license called CC (Common Creatives) that attempts to order the concept of the ownership of ideas inside the cloud. This license authorizes people to copy and redistribute parts of the content and use it for their own gain. However, if someone posts it in a blog with advertising banners, this already characterizes commercial use in a certain sense, which contradicts the CC license. On the other hand, doing the same thing and posting it in a blog without any advertising banners, but which implicitly values the personal image of the person writing it, also characterizes commercial use.

Therefore, neither the "iCloud," "weCloud," or the "ccCloud" represent the origin of our identity. But if we look for the "The-Cloud" on the tabernacle, we will find content of public domain that truly reveals our identity and helps train us for our journey. The domain is public, but it must be ingrained in our life. We need to look for transforming patterns. My entire life, I have sought to identify patterns and I actually see these in objects, people, and situations all the time.

Learning to identify life-wasting patterns has been a very big challenge.

The quality of our life is directly proportional to the standards we establish for ourselves. That is why it is important to challenge negative thought patterns, to think and act positively.

The wrong references pull us down and the correct ones drive us forward.

Science is a pattern; medicine is a pattern; fashion is a pattern; even religion is a pattern.

Every time I try to dissect patterns, I don't do so to try and invalidate them, but rather to try and understand them.

When I was in high school, I had a physics teacher who once said something that intrigued me. He said that there were three great men in the world: Isaac Newton, Albert Einstein, and Jesus Christ.

I didn't understand why he cited the three, but some time later, I came to understand why he cited Newton and then later why he cited Einstein. But Jesus? This one took a while because he does not fit any of the patterns.

If you are able to identify patterns, you will see that life is not a game. But let's pretend that we are playing cards, and each card represented a character in the Bible. You can change the "Who am I card" whenever you want because every character and situation could fit everybody.

The stories in the Bible are a mirror through which we see ourselves, but if I had to find an ace in the hole, I think we could all easily be identified as "Jonahs," running from God at every step!

Just like Jonah, we want to keep ourselves in a comfort zone. In other words, we want to minimize our exposure to risk. That is what life is about. Mine and yours! What we will ultimately discover is that there is far greater uncertainty when it comes to running from God compared to running toward him. God is more interested in defining the boundaries of our character than the boundaries of our comfort zone.

And just as Jonah, I had tried to be someone else, but I finally learned to be myself.

I always tried to research the "faith genome" by attempting to understand my own interactions with the world that extend beyond my physical vision. Deep down right at the start of the journey, the search results from an intuitive feeling we have that God is the product of our upbringing and acquired ideas. Our minds work based on the logic that if we study enough and have the right references, we will have a better understanding of God. But there is one thing that I have learned for certain: nothing escapes his control, and even if I have sought him out for the wrong reason, he will find me for the right one, because God values the search itself:

> ***And you will go on crying to me and making prayer to me, and I will give ear to you. And you will be searching for me and I will be there, when you have gone after me with all your heart.*** **(Jeremiah 29:12–13)**

Why is the heart's intent important? We are what we eat, think, and love. Adoration is a food. We love beauty, fame, status—the truth is that we adore success!

Our individualism demands a servile god. And in order to understand this purpose, the God of the Bible was "re-branded" to be a god that ensures success, and religion delivers the result of this expectation of comfort.

This customized god is the fruit of our own interests and our appetite for worshiping him increases every day. The gospel (marketing) of this god is quite simple; he will give us what we do not have. This is because what we already have becomes obsolete and we no longer need to grow attached to what is not new.

This book will talk more about the process of "debranding"—seeking out the essence and removing all the labels and fads that prompt us to understand God as a supplier and ourselves as the most demanding of clients.

The day finally came that I understood I could no longer pay much attention to my own problems. So, I became the founder and leader of Beit T'Filat Yeshua, a Messianic Jewish congregation that has existed in Rio de Janeiro for almost twelve years. I earned a BA in International Relations and Marketing. I have been researching the "faith genome" since then, and I know that I will not be able to decipher it.

God's mysteries are hidden between our virtues and our vices. He is closer than we may think.

www.debrandinggod.com

CHAPTER 1

DEBRANDING MYSTICISM

Kabbalah . . .

What does Madonna have to do with Kabbalah? Is that even the right question? Coming up with the right question is not easy. Who is Madonna, is not really the most relevant question, but what she represents.

Madonna, the "pop diva," is an icon that influences sexuality, fashion, trends, and even religion. You may not be a fan, but certainly the media bombarded you with the lifestyle that she embodied.

Madonna is a fashion icon that wears religious symbols as part of her character. The trends she started include wearing religious jewelry, bracelets, and headbands.

The cross was one of her most important symbols. A symbol can represent different things. In fact, every symbol is a result of a migration of other symbols that dynamically changed their meaning. A symbol can point beyond itself, to the future or to the past.

The meaning is always more important than the symbol. In comparison with the corporate world, it is very close to the concept of a logo and the brand. Logos are the centerpiece of a company's brand. The logo is a symbol that represents the corporate identity.

What about Madonna? What does the cross represent to her? It certainly is part of the package called Madonna; she is also a brand.

Brand perception is how the public views the product. In Madonna's videos, she did not just wear a cross; she wore a lot of huge crosses. The message Madonna forged is not conservative, but radically opposed. Not all the rebels have a cause, but if they have a cause, they are not alone. They do not care if their ideas are "better," but they do care if they are against the mainstream.

Marketing is not a new ad campaign or this month's promotion. It is intrinsically related to "differentiation" to stand out from the crowd. The message is that the "old" is boring and the "new" is exciting. It has nothing to do with the perception of time, but an attempt to communicate meaningful points of difference.

The pearl is the oyster's masterpiece and at the same time a product. Any art could be a product. Everything is marketing and marketing is everything. Design, fashion, graphics, movies, photos, paintings, cartoons, poetry, music, ideas, sculptures, and even garbage could be art or part of it.

Andy Warhol was probably the most famous artist in the Pop Art movement. Among his most famous works are: *Campbell's Soup Cans* and *Twenty-five Colored Marilyns*.

He transformed cans and celebrity images into commercial art. In fact, Marilyn Monroe was sort of a role model to Madonna. Madonna's look in the "Material Girl" video was a direct copy of Marilyn in *Gentlemen Prefer Blondes*.

One day Madonna said: "You know that we are living in a material world, I am a material girl!" She was right, as any material, the new "Material Girl" was formerly known as Marilyn, and Marilyn is the old style of "Material Girl" who was recycled.

I love to quote the French chemist Antoine Lavoisier who said: *"In nature, nothing is created, nothing is destroyed, and everything is transformed."* Although he was talking about The Law of Conservation of Mass, which explains what happens on an atomic level during a reaction, we certainly could take a philosophical approach. If everything is transformed, we cannot be totally original. There's nothing original under the sun. Even the issues I am bringing to the surface were probably discussed before, and, if you search diligently, you would certainly find that to be true.

I truly believe that if Andy Warhol were alive today, he would be even more successful if he could mix the *Twenty-Five Colored Marilyns* with *Twenty-Five Colored Madonnas* and produce a *Fifty Colored Pop Material Girl Divas*.

Pop Art reflects pop culture. It stands for everything that is commercial and cheap and is accepted as fashionable. Any material, including plastic, bottles, cans, anything disposable and impersonal are the essence of a "new art."

In 2011, I was invited to attend a round table at a university in Rio de Janeiro to discuss environmental marketing. First, all students and professors had to watch the documentary *Waste Land* that was produced by Vik Muniz, a renowned Brazilian artist who lives in Brooklyn, New York. The film documents the life of garbage pickers working at Jardim Gramacho, the world's largest garbage dump located in the outskirts of Rio de Janeiro, which was finally shut down in 2012. Vik Muniz created large-scale mosaic portraits from actual landfill trash that were sold at art auctions in London and exhibited at the museums in Brazil.

During the documentary, Vik Muniz said that the moment of transformation when one thing turns into another is the most beautiful. More important than his art was the effect it had on peoples' lives. Several of the pickers cried when they saw their portraits and realized the beauty of life from another angle. While employed to pick up garbage, they felt like they were garbage. It is very important how you see yourself because it has everything to do with your destiny. It is a terrible way to live when you go through life not liking yourself. Their self-esteem changed and consequently their lives too when they saw themselves working with recyclable material.

This film recycled their lives; suddenly they were portrayed as icons of courage, beauty, and resistance. Every positive new self-image admits that an old negative self-image existed. Against the boring "old," we have the exciting "new," so the "new" is the "old" recycled and packaged in a way that we are able to perceive a desirable future. Madonna did not create her "brand"; only customers can do that. I do not want to confuse the reader with terminology, because in fact, managers and companies create identities all the time. We can create a new name, a new logo, even a new package design, but making those elements a brand depends upon how the audience, the fans, and the media perceive it. We are not in control of a brand, consumers are.

We are always trying to reconstruct ourselves by changing our own rituals of allegiance. That is a way to survive and prove to the world that we are original and unique. The cross for Madonna is not really a form of religious expression.

The cross has been a symbol for Jesus' followers for almost two thousand years. At first, it was not associated with life and resurrection but was a death symbol. The Roman death penalty was accomplished with the cross, and therefore elicited fear. After the Emperor Constantine converted to Christianity in the 4th Century, crucifixion was abolished and the cross became the symbol of Jesus.

Many people think that Jesus invented Christianity and Paul preached it. It is quite an interesting paradox. Christians embraced Jesus as representative of a new religion, but they do not follow the religion Jesus practiced. Jesus was a Jew who practiced Judaism. Paul of Tarsus, a diaspora Jew from Cilicia, whose family came from Galilee, possessed the Pharisaic training and studied under Rabban Gamaliel. He was also a Jew and undoubtedly the most prepared Jewish scholar that announced that Yeshua (Jesus) was the promised Jewish messiah.

Why do religions have symbols? Anyone who works in advertising knows that the use of logos is effective because visual memory is a lot better than any other form of memory. On a spiritual level, the cross, like all religious images, is an icon that ultimately has the purpose of acting as a "window to Heaven," a portal that will open in another dimension beyond the 2-D or 3-D of the logo.

Pablo Picasso, the Spaniard painter, coined a phrase: *Bad artists copy, great artists steal.*

Do not blame Madonna; the truth is that all artists borrow from the work of early pioneers. Actually there are several artists that are copying her and not Marilyn.

She has followers that idolize her. Beyond being an "American Idol," she is actually a "World Idol." It would not be totally crazy to portray her as a priest of a new religion. She is a person but also a character, and certainly she is an idol that is worshipped in the new "Age of Media."

The "Age of Media" is a result of a new era of globalization. The increasing rate of new information being produced is creating some problems like "information overload." Human nature is characterized by the need to create a perpetual factory of idols, and the "Age of Media" allows these idols to be spread globally. We have to understand that information is something we consume, and we have to deal with information overconsumption in the same way we deal with everything that is excessive in our lives. Guy Debord, a French writer and filmmaker, wrote a book entitled *Society of the Spectacle* that basically talks about our "need" to consume information about other's lives.

Why do we care so much about people that we will most likely never meet? What keeps people hungry for more celebrity gossip? All that is missing in the common man's life is supplied by the search of information about actors, politicians, celebrities, gurus, top models, and athletes to provide us a feeling of constant adventure and happiness. Sometimes overconsumption of information does not help us to "find ourselves" but makes us a consumer looking for something new.

People are hungry for a new pattern of beauty, a new philosophy, a new religion, a distinction that promotes them, a difference in lifestyle, and the latest trends of the coolest tribe.

If everything were marketing, religion would not be different. If you trace Christian faith back to its roots, you will find Judaism. Judaism is the religion of Jews, so if you admit that religion is a cultural issue, you can embrace a new culture today and discard the culture the next morning. In other words, you could be a Jew today and a Buddhist tomorrow. But if you see Judaism as an ethnic issue, conversion is far from a simple cultural approach but rather an identity and tribal view.

According to the Polish philosopher Zygmunt Bauman, we are living in a postmodern era that is based upon the concept of "Liquid Modernity." This means that all social relationships are not solid. They move fast in many directions. We tend to not live under the roots. We keep changing and experiencing new values. The world is moving ever more fluid and less solid.

Everything is disposable:
religion, job, and marriage.
If something does not work,
we simply replace it with a new one.

Marriage is no longer an issue of commitment but an issue of status and convenience. Engagement and wedding rings are one of the most popular traditions, but even a "royal wedding" can be transformed into a "royal divorce."

Lawmakers in Mexico City are proposing a new marriage license that would allow couples to split after a two-year trial rather than go through the lengthier divorce process—disposable solutions for disposable commitments that will produce potentially lifelong consequences. Although the foundation of most societies is based on religion, uprooting of these religious roots have occurred. Heritage is being ignored due to media that has become more influential in shaping values.

Religion has become a brand but not necessarily something healthier. The body is now a religious cult, where people go to the gym to work out and buy muscle building products, protein, creatine, diet pills, and equipment in order to worship better. Of course, all of these supplements and devices quickly go to the basement. Additionally, some people prefer objects relating to body parts. That was the case of Imelda Marcos who was the First Lady of the Philippines. The former first lady was famous because 3,000 pairs of shoes were found in the palace's closet, while the rest of the country was living in extreme poverty.

The luxury and sophistication of today will be the need of tomorrow. The excluded of today are the consumers of the future. Tensions and stresses of today are more related to consumption than beliefs.

The Cartesian maxim says: *"I think, therefore I am."* But it has been replaced by the new liquid modernity maxim: *"I shop, therefore I am.*" I am not a hypocrite to say that I live in a transcendent dimension, hating consumerism. We all live in a consumer society and we have to accept that.

I truly believe that if Brad Pitt and Angelina Jolie decided to create a religion, thousands of people would be born again and baptized according to their rituals only to have them as priests.

The truth is that religion has increasingly become a luxury item, sold at a fancy store by attractive sales professionals, as if it were a brand of Rolex watches or Louis Vuitton purses. Although religion has always been an instrument of social affirmation and used for political purposes, today the status is more related to personal marketing.

The "Age of Media" is the age of the "Society of the Spectacle" where millions of people chose to live their lives through others. For this society, a religious conviction is like a fashion accessory that will be a trend. As tattoos are now a mainstream fashion accessory for men and women, religious faith is always something very important in the "pop icon culture bundle."

Some people say that Kabbalah is a practice not a religion. Although it springs from Judaism, there are roots in many cultures. Sometime owning a market means broadening it, other times narrowing it. If religion is a mass marketing tool, Kabbalah is a narrow segment without the necessity to impose moral and ethical pressure on their followers.

Kabbalah dates back to the medieval age, when the *Zohar* was published. Interestingly, Jewish mysticism has gone up and down over the centuries, and it is currently experiencing a big upswing in attention as celebrities have started practicing a form of it.

We see over and over in the *Tanakh* (Old Testament) that the Hebrew people fell from obeying the Torah and embraced witchcraft and sorcery. The spiritual life of Israel was like a roller coaster ride, up and down all the time. We encounter their obedience, disobedience, repentance, and constant struggle to remain faithful to God and the Torah.

There are many motivations that attract people to religion. Understanding the meaning of life and the fear of death are among the "spiritual needs." They could be combined with "psychological needs" which include honor, idealism, curiosity, and acceptance. We can include the "pragmatic needs," which is another approach that establishes religion as a way to prosperity.

We select our motivations instinctively according to our own true nature. We can get involved seeking mystical experiences, or through an intellectual bias, or even by being pragmatic.

Our differences—in personality as well as life experience—matter. Life is always packed with struggles, troubles, trials, hard work, sweat, tears, and pain. Oftentimes we wish we had a magic wand to void these harder times in life.

People want to be a new wizard at Hogwarts with ancient magic. Beware, every Harry Potter magical wand will break, and even if you fix it with scotch tape you will not be able to find the real truth.

The problem with a mystical experience is that in mysticism each is his own prophet. A prophet that instead of connecting to God connects with the present. The mystic has no hope because he does not admit that the future will cooperate with him without his intervention. His life is a total immersion in the present; his spells work only to modify the present and he does not have the slightest idea how they will harm his future. Do not worry; "mysticism" is not a bad word. It means supernatural. It is something that is not natural; it cannot be explained by science. Every religion works at a mystical level.

Jewish mysticism began in biblical days, long before the term Kabbalah was "branded." Why should you care about it? Mysticism? Hocus-Pocus stuff? Voodoo? New age? Esoteric Jewish philosophy?

The word Kabbalah comes from a Hebrew root meaning "to receive." Every Friday night is the beginning of the Shabbat. That is why Kabbalat Shabbat means, "receiving the Shabbat."

If you arrive at a hotel in Israel, the hotel receptionist who works at the front desk greeting guests upon arrival and assisting them with any problems during their stay works at the Kabbalah (the Hebrew name for reception).

Kabbalah, as some understand it today, is a new package with different content. It can appear that inside the box there is an amalgam of paganism and philosophy that deviates from the Torah. Some alter the view of Kabbalah from its traditional context this way because they are not pursuing the truth; they are chasing the power. They are producing their own truth, repackaging an old era in a new age.

If mysticism has one great tool, it's mysteriousness. People are fascinated with mystery. Men are attracted to women with confidence and that presents a mystery. We love secret formulas for success, the secret formula for losing weight, or even an ancient hair-growing formula.

You can pack anything you want: from fresh eggs to a huge elephant, from mysticism to Judaism, from Torah to Christianity, from oral tradition to Kabbalah, from Marilyn to Madonna, and from Nostradamus to several soap opera magazines.

Adding the element of mystery is essential in a brand "new" package. We can find in any religion the good, the not so good, and what is still missing.

***

When we recall the word "mystic," we are thinking about people who have supernatural experiences, visions, and other spiritual gifts. Mystical experiences are related in the Bible. In fact, that is the most mystical book of all time. Every epiphany is a mystical experience. Moses had his epiphany, as did Elijah, Isaac, and David. Israel had his during a 40-year journey through the desert.

Life is an unpredictable journey. Is it about time to roll up for a mystery journey? *Magical Mystery Tour,* a song by the Beatles, consists of mainly two lines of lyrics: "roll up for the mystery tour" and "the magical mystery tour is waiting to take you away." Some argue that these lyrics are completely meaningless. However, there is a magical mystery tour bus in Liverpool, which was the hometown of the Beatles.

We can go beyond the world's most exciting cities. Our tour is not limited to Liverpool, Paris, New York, Jerusalem, or even to a small village in Eastern Europe. We are explorers of time and space. We seek the meaning of life over distances and time. Our focus is telescopic, rarely is it microscopic.

With the telescope we can shorten distances and observe in detail the seas, rivers, valleys, stars, and the moon. With the microscope, the understanding of life changes the focus. The microscope searches what is small in the cell, in a blood drop, in a crystal salt, the small insect, in what is seemingly insignificant, and the response that the focus of large distances cannot see.

What is infinitely large and infinitely small is what keeps secrets and treasures that only the most attentive explorers realize. Where does the telescope end and the microscope begin? Which one do you see more?

Both can see a lot but with a different focus. There's a

sequence because the telescopic focus is only balanced with the microscopic look when time starts to weigh on life's journey. The maturity and growth open up the microscopic focus that we need.

A true explorer does not get stuck with their eye at the telescope. He will also need a microscope focused on himself in order to explore the hidden secrets during life's journey.

Although the journey orchestrated by God is not always strictly linear, it is a safe trip. The mystic desires to be as close to God as possible, to be part of the divine but searches for power without commitment to his word, which is what would make his trip dangerous.

We have few choices. If we cannot trust God, then we need to trust in our own power.

God is a relational God. I believe his main activity is to build relationships. It is amazing how he reveals himself and establishes a relationship on a personal level. It means that we should not have expectations that he will relate with us in the very same way he does with someone else.

A relationship with him cannot be imitated and he has no competitors. The bottom line of this unique relationship is communication. Many people, in order to facilitate this interaction, prefer to get outside the box of the religious system and decide to build their own, new box. Every time we divide the attributes of creation in pieces, we worship the part and not the fullness of the blessings.

We can either choose to live for our work, or work to live. If we live to obtain the joy of money, and that's the main goal in life, we have fragmented our life in only one piece. If life is reduced to marriage, a bad marriage means a broken life.

If everything is attached to a single piece of life we live a partial life.

People that worship the sun and the moon are labeled as pagans. "Paganism" happens when instead of worshiping the creator, we decide to worship the creation. Based upon this concept, we are no longer different from pagans.

Marriage, work, sun, and moon are good things. Everything created by God reveals him. But when we restrain our life to small pieces we have an idolater attitude.

If we continue breaking God and the creation in pieces, we will never complete the puzzle. If we do not try to understand the word of God as a whole process in a relationship, then we risk turning Kabbalah and other tools into paganism. Paul understood this concept, and the New Testament does not disconnect from the goal, which is to establish the Malchut (Kingdom) through the right way.

Walking a road implies decisions. Every move will have certain consequences on your life. You can be sure you will run into delays, roadblocks, detours, U-turns, and dead ends along the way. Proverbs 14:12 says:

> ***There is a way that seems right to a man,***
> ***but its end is the way to death.***

God does not always take us the fast way or the easy way. He knows where every road is leading and where the dead ends are. So he wants to teach us the right path.

Rent a car service is very popular in many western countries, but especially in the United States. I travelled several times to the US and I can tell through my own experience that renting a car is essential; public transportation is not sufficient and taxis are expensive.

Not many years ago, the rental car agency provided us free paper roadmaps. However, in recent years the maps talk to us. Perhaps people do not realize how GPS is a revolutionary device. Think about it, now the maps literally speak to the driver. Amazing technology!

Where are you headed on life's road? How do you know which way to go? Your Creator offers a high-tech roadmap. He talks to us!

This will only happen when we leave aside all of our self-sufficiency and trust in the sufficiency from God in order to transform ourselves into that which he has planned.

If you are still in doubt, I suggest that you start to pray. The act of praying is fundamentally associated with the need to focus our decisions based on God's will. That is why we pray—to align our will with the permission from God. What is interesting is that there is a great spiritual secret guaranteeing us that when there is resonance between man and God, our desire is realized.

Paul said: ***Test everything; retain what is good.***

Certainly, he was not saying that we could "test-drive" a religion for a month. All of Paul's statements come from a holistic view of human beings and their need to pursue information.

Living in a media-driven culture, we can understand this point easily. Do people search and research Islam, Buddhism, or Kabbalah to quench their spiritual thirst, or are they really trying to brand their identity?

Yes Madonna, you missed the point!

CHAPTER 2

UNLOCKING YOUR DNA

Nothing is "immobile;" everything is in motion. Nothing is stagnant; everything moves; everything vibrates. The study of movement is a required step for learning any scientific area. Cinematics is what the area of Physics calls the study of movements without a concern for analyzing their causes. The movement will always be directly proportional to the speed, which is measured in function of time.

Every movement and every journey must be measured by a clock. In fact, the main cause of our concerns is always connected to time—the clock imprisons and the clock frees. The absence of haste frees us, and on the other hand, the anxiety and anguish of running against the clock enslaves us. The clock seems to have a soul. If it helps us, then it is certainly our friend. However, if it gets in our way, we consider it an enemy. And there is no sense in stopping the clock's hands, since there will always be others to mark out the time we prefer to ignore. After all, we live in a world full of clocks. The clock has even become a sort of god in our modern times.

However, the clock is not only a god of our own century, since even Greek mythology had already spoken of this divinity—with Chronos (sometimes transliterated as *Khronos*), who is the personification of time. The root of the words chronology, chronic, and chronometer come from the Greek word *khronos,* meaning "time." He controlled the rotation of the skies and the eternal course of time. Later, another Cronus emerged. This one appeared during another time and was classified as a Titan. Violent and aggressive, he was a god who devoured the life of his own children.

It is, in fact, impossible to run away from time. All creatures will end up being devoured by it one way or another. And we are devoured regardless of our geographic location. Whether we're in a major urban metropolis or some lost isolated island, this cannibalism still occurs. Even based on the stories of castaways who lived isolated from the rest of the world, far from civilization, measuring time was a way of staying sane (or prompting insanity). For them, time was measured based on astronomic events, such as the rotation of the Earth or the different phases of the moon.

It's not only for castaways; human civilization has always sought to count time, since the earliest eras using this simple way of counting days. However, this did not solve the problem of counting semi-intervals such as hours and minutes. It did not take long for men who counted days to create clepsydras (water clocks), hourglasses (sand clocks), and pendulum and rope clocks. Today, it is the atomic clock that tells time. Technological advances use increasingly more precise synchronisms.

However, clocks are still a source of fascination even today and can be found on the wrists of everyone from the humblest souls to the wealthiest. The truth is that no one buys some famous brand name watch made of pure gold because it tells time better than some simple mass-made digital watch. People buy based on status.

Of course it is not real, but it is like so many "surrealities." A truly assumed Surrealist was Spanish painter Salvador Dali, who said that the difference between he and the surrealists was that he was surrealism embodied.

Born in Catalonia in 1904, Salvador Dali was given the same name as an older brother who had died three years earlier from meningitis. The fact that as a child, he was forced to take flowers to a tomb of someone who had his own name caused in him a supposed emotional instability, since there was one Salvador Dali that was dead and another alive. He referred to the Dali from the tomb as his *"otro yo"* (other me).

Time is what separates death from life. Maybe that is why Salvador Dali was obsessed with clocks. An eccentric and controversial artist, one of his paintings is called *Persistence of Memory* (also known as *Soft Watches*). The theme of the painting is time represented by the three watches, which represent the past, present, and future. However, these watches appear to be melted, flexible, malleable, seeming almost to flow along the surface that supports them. Whether or not influenced by Einstein, Dali already understood the dilatation of time, where it is no longer rigid or absolute.

The devotion of time is notorious. In the New Year's celebrations held around the world, one of the palpable traits is the feeling of hope and adoration for a festivity that actually involves revering and hailing the transition from the last second of one year that is ending to the first moment of a year that begins. Time is celebrated as if it had a soul and the power to determine the future. And this god of time is not only celebrated on the Greek Olympus, but rather worldwide.

Being in London on New Year's Eve means partying at midnight at the time that defines all the celebrations around the world. In the prime meridian city of Greenwich, a reference for time around the globe, the people of London celebrate the New Year. The main fireworks show takes place at the banks of the Thames River, with Westminster Palace setting the scenery and the sounds of the chimes of the Big Ben Clock, the world's most famous, with the London Eye Ferris wheel in the background. As always, the famous British punctuality helps instill the new myth of the faith in time.

It is no different in the United States. When counting down the final moments of the year, thousands of tourists gather at Times Square in New York with their eyes glued to the clock, waiting for the descent of that famous multi-colored ball. They wait hours under snow, rain, and glacial cold to witness the last seconds of the year, when they finally cry out with joy under the confetti rain.

In Rio de Janeiro, Brazil, in the sweltering heat of the tropics on Copacabana Beach, two million people wearing white amass along the shoreline, in the company of thousands of others onboard cruise ships anchored out at sea. There are several stages on the beach with synchronized shows preceding the countdown, with several floating barges in the background filled with fireworks, awaiting the moment to celebrate the ritual of a new year.

In elegant Paris, the crowd celebrates the ritual of time at the feet of the Eiffel Tower, complete with lights and musical performances. In Germany, hundreds of thousands of people meet up at the Brandenburg Portal to commemorate the birth of yet another year.

Regardless of the site, time is people's focus. The final countdown of those last instants of December 31 is the same, regardless of the language: 10, 9, 8, 7, 6, 5, 4, 3, 2, 1 … and then everyone shares the mutual desire: HAPPY NEW YEAR!

The passage of the New Year represents the end of one cycle and the start of another. Not just the simple change of a digit on the calendar. It is a moment that is always brimming with dreams and resolutions. A Shamanic ritual, where the rituals feed the dreams and breathe life into the celebrations. Everyone decides that for this year that is beginning, they will do everything that they did not do last year. They remember to take that course, try to care for their health and their body. They wish for a new house, a new car, a wedding, an unforgettable trip, a promotion at work, a child, the list is endless.

The following year, the trance continues. The fireworks explode again in different places around the world and time is revered yet again! But what is this time?

Another clock exists, because there is another type of time. The ancient Greeks had two words for time: *chronos* (whose name was already explained by Greek mythology) and *kairos*. While the first refers to chronological or sequential time, this last one is a moment during which something special happens. It is the right time, the opportune time. *Kairos* describes the qualitative form of time, the "time of God," while *chronos* is of a quantitative nature, the "time of men."

Hebrew, the original language of the Torah, includes some interesting secrets about this concept. In addition to linear time, there is also a cyclical time. Chapter 23 of the Book of

Leviticus talks about a time that repeats itself and which is simultaneously an appointment for meeting with God. The traditional festivities and important ceremonies are called *moed* in the singular and *moadim* in the plural, which establish a meeting.

It is important to observe that while Salomon in Jerusalem had not yet built the permanent temple, there was a mobile tabernacle also known as *mishkan*. He moved about in the middle of the desert and within it, there was a meeting point where the presence of God could be felt. It was known as the meeting tent, or in Hebrew, *Ohel Moed*.

What an interesting thing: the word *moed* is used to indicate a site, but also refers to time—so there was a meeting in time!

Because nothing is immobile, everything is movement, we will enter a time machine and seek to better understand Jacob's journey.

Jacob was a privileged man. He had opportunities and did not waste them. He knew that the secret to victory was found in God.

He persevered. He was obsessed with this. He forced out his father's blessing and went in search of God's blessing. The truth is that he forced a sort of collision with God. He knew that this was his only chance for survival.

The story began like this: Loved by his mother, blessed by his father, and hated by his brother, Jacob fled to try and save his own skin. His twin brother Esau was furious to learn he had been tricked.

Because Jacob left his parents' home in such a hurry, he did not have time to prepare his baggage. Perhaps he even left only with the clothing on his own back and the few supplies prepared by his mother at the last minute. That is when the fight for his life began. After walking hours on end, Jacob reached a small town called Luz. Night had fallen, and everyone was already asleep. Trying to avoid calling too much attention to himself, Jacob preferred to sleep outside. He found a rock, turned it into a pillow and fell into a deep sleep.

That was when he had an experience that would mark his life. He dreamed of a ladder and angels that climbed up and down it through a portal carved out in the heavens.

Perhaps it was at that very moment that Jacob came into contact with the faith genome. After all, the DNA structure does resemble a helical ladder containing the genetic instructions that coordinate how all living beings function. The DNA of Jacob's faith begins to be revealed at that moment.

It's time to wake up! And Jacob awoke.

> ***As he awoke from his dream, Jacob said: The Lord is actually here at this place, and I did not know it***

The vision has such a big effect on him that he called the site Bethel (house of God) where he saw *Shaar Hashamaim* (portal of the Heavens).

It was the awakening of a new awareness—the awareness of the divine. For a man so set on finding a spiritual meaning to his life, there is nothing worse than losing the awareness of God's presence.

Before Jacob got there, God was already waiting. He does not inhabit temples made by human hands. He does not fit within the geographic limits of a specific region. Not even the heaven of the heavens can contain him.

He is also not exclusive of any religion. He is not Catholic, or Protestant, or Jewish. He is God! There is no place in the universe where he cannot be found.

The House of God is where we can feel his presence. However, certainly the focus is not "where" we felt his presence, but rather "when" we felt it. It doesn't matter whether we are in a cave, atop Mt. Everest, inside a tunnel, or in a church. Once human awareness is awakened, the House of God appears there. This is the moment of its manifestation.

But even the start of awareness occurs with varied and growing intensities. We are always awakening. Jacob's time and God's time crossed. There was an intersection between two timelines. When the "*chronus line*" and the "*kairos line*" intercept, we have a *moed*, a meeting, or in other words, a miracle!

Nevertheless, we do not have a joining of two lines that are linear, but rather a function, curved, complex, and impossible to modulate mathematically. There is no differential and integral calculation that approximates this function to some known model, but certainly this intersection exists and is not governed by causality.

Jacob's journey does not end there in Bethel. Time goes by and 20 years later, the function works again and another meeting will take place. Jacob is very nervous because he will have to face his brother and seek reconciliation. Esau has 400 heavily armed men and Jacob is at the height of his stress, fearing for the life of his children and wives.

The night arrived heavy, dense, and dark and the moon shone shyly, seeming to hide between the clouds. Jacob was tense, breathless, and worried. He (hopelessly) saw his life passing by like a movie in his head. Memories of his childhood, of his beloved mother, and his strict, but dedicated father. He could not forget his dear father. The image of the deathbed came to his head.

—*Who are you*? asked the father. The same question that was asked 20 years ago.

—*I am Esau!* The same answer …

Jacob spent his entire life wanting to be someone else, but now he becomes himself. He is not Esau. He must come to an understanding with his "other me," his twin that pursued him.

The dawn arrived, and his children and wives had already crossed the Yabok River. He remained alone. He needed to stay alone. It was a crucial moment in his life. He remembered everything that he had gone through during all those years. He remembered how he met his wives, his father-in-law, his children, and his journey.

He was returning to point zero, the point of departure. He could hardly know that his journey had only just begun. His mind whirled, when suddenly he found a man. Jacob was ready for anything. It was meeting time—either for life or death. But he knew that this was no common man. Something fantastic was about to happen.

Jacob was a warrior, and like any good warrior, he is ready to fight. He grabs the angel and says:

—*Bless me!*

—*Release me. I must go!* responds the angel.

—*I will not release you until you bless me!*

—*Release me as I have asked.*

Jacob does not obey and as such, the angel strikes him on the thigh, leaving a scar he will carry for the rest of his life.

—*Tell me know, what is your name?* asked the angel.

—*Yaacov! Yaacov! That is my name!*

Jacob weeps. He repents. He depletes himself. From this moment forward, he was no longer Esau. This time, he was sincere. In the presence of God, he did not wish to pretend to be another. He was authentic. He was himself, wearing no masks.

The angel then said:

—*You are no longer called Jacob, but Israel, because you battled with God and with men and you prevailed!*

This was the longest dawn of Jacob's life. The sun began to rise. Those who thought that his journey was drawing to an end received a big surprise—the journey was merely beginning.

He started to walk with a limp, a sign of what had happened. Furthermore, this sign was neither for friends nor enemies to realize that he had changed. No! It was so Jacob himself would never forget that God had changed his life, in all areas, and he was now Israel. He who had won because he hoisted the white flag and allowed himself to be defeated.

Once again, the paths of *chronus* and *kairos* crossed, and this time, Jacob called the site Peniel, which means: "I saw God, face-to-face."

However, Jacob did not find his great confront with Esau, but rather with God. The key to decoding the faith genome is for us to be rid of our lies, presumptions, and deformed convictions and submit ourselves to God because our defeating him will never be a possibility.

The confrontation was inevitable and perhaps Jacob's biggest virtue was that he sought out this battle and did not put off the inevitable. He was fully aware that he was a "spiritual being" and was sensible to the presence of a power and favor that came from God.

Take note that in the middle of the fight, the angel's question to the prince appears to be naive and insignificant, but therein lies a secret. The secret is that nothing can be hidden from the eyes of God. Twenty years ago, Jacob entered the tent of his father—blind and dying—who asked his name and he responded:

I am Esau!

Now, 20 year later, the angel asked the same question that Isaac had. The difference is that this time, the answer was sincere. In the presence of God, Jacob did not wish to pretend to be another. He was authentic. He was himself, wearing no masks. All masks will crumble one day. God only appears before us when we are before him in our most authentic form.

God gave Jacob the opportunity to rid himself of all deformed character, and introduces in him a new one. He is transformed into Israel, he who prevails above everything and everyone due to his truth and spiritual determination.

Jacob is the archetype of every human being, with his weaknesses and virtues, intermingled with so many doubts. The doubt between being himself and the one that deep down inside, he envied. There is a duality within us.

My theory is that we all have a twin. We just have not found it yet. This twin is wandering around somewhere on planet Earth. Esau was Jacob's alter ego. He actually wanted to be Esau his entire life, until he finally gave up on trying to be someone else and accepted his own journey, assuming the role of being himself. The truth is that he wanted his brother's blessing because he did not like his own life.

I myself have undergone this process. I gave up trying to be another and decided to be myself. Every time we compare ourselves to others, we lose the gift of savoring life because we want to live someone else's life, taking the journey of another instead of embarking on our own.

It is actually a great insult to God to want to be another person, because when we refuse to accept our own journey, when we refuse to be who we are, we are telling God that he made a mistake. We actually trade places with him and wish to redesign our body, rework our characteristics, add new talents, and suppress that which does not please us. We want to be rich, beautiful, healthy, and famous, all in the hopes that this will make us happy.

But God did not get it wrong. God did not make anyone inferior or second-class. All of us are a masterpiece, potentially destined for success with unique and exclusive characteristics.

That is why it is so important to further develop this faith genome, becoming excited about your personality, life, and appearance because no one will be a "me" equal to you. You are the best "me" that exists!

You are unique and must truly believe that nothing happens by chance. The difference that lies within you is asking permission to show itself to the world. Just as Jacob's story does not end in Peniel (it was just beginning), yours is also not over and it may even be that it has not yet even begun. Allow this difference to reveal itself.

CHAPTER 3

BUILDING LOYALTY

Some people say that trust is the base of any relationship. Others alternate between honesty, respect, transparency, and the capacity to establish communication.

Undoubtedly, all are important ingredients. After all, they will generate loyalty. Differentiating things that are so similar, and which even complete each other and are easily confused, is a complex task.

Betrayal moves in the opposite direction of commitment. Being faithful, above all, means being loyal to alliances, being loyal to relationships, and being loyal to common objectives despite the obstacles. Betrayal is the consequence of a weakening of the bond between the parties. If the conflicts outweigh the bonds that hold the relationship together, the rupture will be inevitable.

We want everything that is good to last as long as possible. That is why a good relationship is something that is lasting. Loyalty building is a relationship process that is under continuous construction, since our values are also being constantly constructed. The dynamics of life generate a dynamic to relationships. A person who has been married for

15 years is not the same person now as when he or she walked down the aisle and committed to a relationship.

Loyalty building is generally confused with satisfaction, but satisfaction is momentary and loyalty building is a long term contract in which satisfaction is expected.

When brought down to a daily level, loyalty building is about maintaining relationships, firming up alliances, and above all, not allowing space for the threats made by new "players," or in other words, avoiding competition at all costs.

In the case of the couple, there is nothing more frightening than the possibility that one will seek out other experiences. After all, if such experiences are more satisfactory, they will most certainly weaken the bonds that hold the relationship together. For specialists in marketing, loyalty building is a concept that seeks to minimize the possibility that the customer will look for new suppliers and alternatives.

Valentine's Day is a typical example of an event that explores the concept of loyalty building on several different levels. The emotional sense is symbolized on the official day, and the couples know that if they consider the date to be irrelevant, they may lose opportunities to strengthen bonds and end up weakening the union because they placed socially accepted values in doubt.

In the commercial sense, the date serves as the opportunity for merchants to attract new customers and seek to increase the retention rates for their longer-term clients. However, the loyalty building relationship between suppliers and customers is very pragmatic, since nobody will be faithful to a company just to be faithful, but rather because they want some advantage out of this relationship.

From the perspective of the couples, the kisses and declarations of eternal love, exchanges of cards, boxes of chocolates and gifts, make it clear that the loyalty building that really counts is that which keeps the bonds of the emotional relationships strong.

There is even a marketing specialty called relationship marketing that covers the concepts of loyalty and its goal is to build the customer's loyalty. That is why there are tools like CRM (Customer Relationship Management), which is actually a process that transforms data into information, helping the company sell the right products, at the right time, to its clientele.

The name is sophisticated, but it is no different than the owner of the old neighborhood warehouse, who got to know his customers personally and, therefore, could predict their consumption habits. The commercial relationship was also based on a personal relationship, one capable of producing bonds and predictability.

Satisfaction is something real, but yet still a subjective concept that is very hard to measure because it is the customer's perception of value. Loyalty building in marketing is the result of repeated purchases.

It is common to hear that a satisfied customer speaks to one, while an unsatisfied one speaks to 10. Satisfaction can be subjective, but dissatisfaction is very real. It has destructive effects. In a world so connected and brimming with social networks, critique becomes lethal. After all, one can now speak to thousands and not just to 10.

A deteriorated relationship contaminates others, which will fail to create bonds due to the expectation for failure. The breaking of trust happens during the embryonic phase, even before the relationship exists.

Preserving a good relationship is essential, but conflict is inherent to relationships. Conflict is part of the relationship itself, and if there are still no differing opinions and stressful moments, then the relationship did not develop properly. The conflict emerges when there is the need to choose between situations that may be considered incompatible.

How does this work when it comes to our spiritual life? Good seeks a relationship, but the methodology of this relationship cannot be measured or systematized.

The relationship with God does not need to be "Liked" in the social networks and much less does it require tools to monitor its satisfaction rates.

Let's take a journey in a fictitious time machine and adjust our coordinates to the remote past. Understanding the base of everything helps us understand the present. The base of the relationship between man and God always occurred at the *Mizbeach* (altar). By definition, the altar is a place of sacrifice that allows for the establishment of the relationship. The "I" is diminished, the base of all conflict, and there is an assumption of dependence, compliance, and pardon related to the "I AM."

There is one important observation here. "I AM" is how God identifies himself to Moses after a very objective question. This is exactly how it is written in Exodus 3:13-14:

> ***Moses said to God, When I come to the children of Israel and say to them, the God of your fathers has sent me to you: and they say to me, What is his name? What am I to say to them? And God said to him, I***

AM WHAT I AM: and he said, Say to the children of Israel, I AM has sent me to you.

An abstract and subjective concept for Moses to understand at first, but a reality capable of freeing an enslaved people from chains and whips, capable of making the impossible possible, of generating transformation. The real world does not limit God, or language, or the alphabet. Accordingly, a simple name could not describe him.

A name is not a simple label, but rather represents the true essence of that to which it belongs. The act of naming something indicates belonging, being within the reach of its understanding, and being under its influence.

When man perceives what is going on around him, he immediately begins to conceptualize. This human vocation was created at the same time that man himself was created. Whether right or wrong, the surrounding universe is a conceptualization based on the perception by a man whose mind is not without its limits. Man himself struggles to understand, since indetermination troubles him. That is why he always seeks to establish definitions.

Defining God is a troubling task, since he is not a concept based on the perception of the one who perceives. God allows himself to be perceived, but human perception does not define him. God does not die, since he does not live in the interval of time. God inhabits, but does not need space. He is unchanging, indifferent to time and space. He exists, he declares: I AM! He has always existed, even before we began to conceptualize the world.

Indeed, Hebrew holds some interesting secrets because it is a language that reflects God's nature in details. Although the verb "to be" exists in Hebrew, it is used only extremely rarely in written text. For a very simple reason in the Hebrew culture, no man "is." He may have been in the past or will be in the future, but only God "is" in the present. Only God is; only God possesses, which shows that all of our existence depends exclusively on that which in fact is the only thing that "is," the only one who "possesses" everything. This is a surprising revelation, since even though we have acquired goods through the effort of our work, only he possesses, and accordingly, our sustenance depends directly on him. And even more than this, God is our salvation, our life force, our health, and our children. Everything belongs to him. He is sovereign. Only he "has." Only he "IS."

It is precisely this "I AM" that wants to reveal itself to the "I." And this act is consummated fully at the altar.

The first altar builder in the Torah was Noah. He understood a great deal about the need to create a point of physical contact that would serve as a milestone in a relationship. The site is important, but without the mortification of the "I." The construction of the altar becomes merely an architectural construction.

Noah built the first altar after the great flood, which was a storm of overwhelming proportions; waters exploded from the earth and poured violently from the skies. The altar that was built had a clear objective—it was made to express proximity.

Nothing in Creation occurs by chance. The first thing that the children of Israel were oriented to do when they returned from exile in Babylon was to rebuild the temple and raise the altar. After all, the temple is a structure that houses the altar. It is literally a sacred house, since the return from exile clearly shows that the relationship is the number one priority on God's agenda.

Exile is the result of a distancing. When man wants distance, God then allows him to live distantly, without a temple, without an altar, without life, without purpose, and worse of all, entirely at his own will.

When man's will is to live self-sufficiently, he lives in the "I," or in other words, he lives exiled from the will of "I AM."

From a human perspective, God's logic is a reverse logic to the values of "I" and that is why they are so hard to accept. If it depended on our own agenda, things would be quite different. The human perspective is based on the premises that the most important thing is to erect walls to protect us from enemies. The next step is to build a home to live in, and finally the process is completed by raising the altar. However, the sequence established by God reverses everything, since the people of Israel first built the altar, then the home, and finally, raised the walls.

The return from exile and construction of the temple were not easy tasks. It was work that demanded a great deal of effort and resources. Despite its success, the human engineering was pushed into the background, since the true masterpiece was created in the field of spiritual engineering. Building the altar is work that requires patience, humbleness, and the resolution of conflicts, submission, harmony, and transparency.

The conclusion that one arrives at is that the altar is much more effective as protection against enemies than are walls. It is the beginning of everything. The relationship with God is based on constructing and maintaining this altar. Maintaining the altar is indeed a start to loyalty building.

The burning question is: What should we do at the altar?

Technically speaking, the altar is a site where blood is spilled. Sacrifice serves to bring life, abundant and complete. Life is represented by blood. However, sprinkling blood over the altar is fundamentally an action intended to claim life.

Life is found in blood, and it circulates throughout the entire body through the vascular system to give the body oxygen, $CO_{2,}$ and nutrients. That is why when we go see the doctor, he or she may ask us to take a trip to the laboratory to check our triglycerides, cholesterol, blood sugar, and blood pressure—to discover the perfect medication to prescribe to keep us healthy.

And when we lose blood during surgery, a blood transfusion becomes necessary to restore life. To create an analogy, the altar is a site where the spiritual surgical procedure occurs, but the blood transfusion exists because just as sin is not something virtual, neither is blood.

One of the most delicate surgeries practiced in modern medicine is the heart transplant. It is only used as a last resort, when all other alternatives have already been exhausted. And to make matters even more complicated, a donor is still needed.

This surgery requires the surgeon to literally "open" the heart, and in the spiritual world, the heart means the altar. In fact, the altar indicates proximity, and the closest altar is the one that exists in our own heart. And we must be willing to open our heart to be operated.

Opening the heart causes some pain, but not opening it brings about death.

The opposite of life is death, and without a relationship with God, we die because when we separate ourselves from the source of life, we draw closer to death. The heart is designed to pump blood. Blood also carries toxins. It was created to transport life, and when we are healthy, this is exactly what it does. But when we are not healthy, it can transport death. Sin is a toxin. It causes death. It is a barrier to the relationship with God and therefore, it must be removed not as an option, but as a need. That is why nobody is free from this transfusion.

Pardon is the foundation of the relationship and it is built with an altar, sacrifice, and blood. It is not built with walls, homes, CRM tools, advertising, religions, or philosophies.

Another interesting aspect of the altar is that a holocaust was burned on it and its smoke reached the skies. This reminds me a lot of the old Western movies starring John Wayne, where the smoke signals were used by tribes of Indians that alternated between short and long signals. Despite its rudimentary nature, the method worked. The technology evolved, but the principle remained the same. The telegraph, invented in 1835 by Samuel Morse, created a binary writing code that used electric signals to express points and dashes, or short and long signals. The acclaimed S.O.S. message was written to facilitate Morse code to warn when a ship was in danger.

Leonardo da Vinci said that simplicity is the ultimate sophistication. The current technology of computers is a digital smoke signal. After all, it is no more than a binary language that uses the very same principle. The byte that forms a character is made up of a state of "on" or "off," which is indicated by a 0 or 1. There are only two options. Simple, right?

God reads S.O.S. in all codes—whether through smoke, telegraph, or digital binary codes. But he goes far beyond media and sophistication because he reads hearts. It does not matter whether the technology is rudimentary or modern. What matters is not the media, but rather the implicit content of the message, because it sees beyond the codes. God is the reader of hearts!

Every offer is delivery. Therefore, it is based on the principle that there is an act of delivery. The delivery cannot be partial, just as a smoke signal, Morse code, or a digital binary message cannot be truncated in half. If there is no remorse, there is no truth. If there is no truth, there is no transparency. Those who want intimacy and a complete relationship surrender themselves entirely and not partially.

Do not think it's easy to let go of your control over life, your problems, concerns, fear, sadness, and pride and enter 100% completely in God's presence. One can only enter completely through dependence, and our tendency toward independence generates conflict in this relationship.

Every delivery on the altar leaves some debris. Part of the sacerdotal function is the act of collecting all the ashes left over at the altar, literally sweeping up the dirt. All the dirt has to be thrown out. If we don't do this in our homes, tossing out the leftover food and throwing all the garbage away, the house will start to smell bad.

Certain things in our lives are so commonplace that we don't pay any attention. Have you stopped to think that we live in a city where there are people who work to collect our garbage? Isn't it incredible that there is someone out there cleaning up our mess? This is basically what the garbage collectors do—they collect the waste of our consumption and the mess from our homes. How many people would want to be in their shoes? It's hard enough as it is taking care of our own mess, much less that of others. They don't allow you to build up the garbage from your life.

That's exactly what the priest does. He did it happily, without complaining, because if he did it complaining, he also would not be complete before the altar. The priest's duty was full of royalty and even his clothing expressed this. His work included removing the ashes; he needed to be humble and committed.

The blood on the altar symbolizes life, and the only things left over from the renewal of life are the ashes of the burned holocaust. That which died within us gave us life. The residue must be cleaned every day, since we leave such waste behind daily.

Every mother knows the trick to cleaning up the mess on the kitchen table. She knows that if her child spills soup, yogurt, chocolate milk, or any sticky substance on the table, that the key to cleaning is to act immediately. Clean it before it sticks for good!

Let this serve as a lesson to us all. Cleaning is something that should be done with seriousness and urgency. The Torah is full of commandments but lacks suggestions. Commandments are orders and an order is something that drives you, that gets you ready, not for the routine, but for a reawakening. It is interesting that the Passover ceremony, which is celebrated in remembrance of the exodus from Egypt, prohibits you from eating leavened foods for seven days. In one of his statements, even Yeshua associated leaven with sin, leaving no doubt about this order. Until today, Orthodox Jewish families followed this orientation strictly by removing *Hametz* (leaven) from their homes. Actually, this is the first step preceding Passover, called

Bedikat Hametz in Hebrew, or the removal of all leavened foods from the homes.

The symbolism is obviously important, but the message is clear—the symbolism points to the reality. Nothing can be incomplete. It is necessary to remove a piece of life. That is why the altar is the site where life is claimed.

The dictionary defines routine as the path normally taken; the habit of always doing something the same way; a monotonous repetition of the same things. Spiritual beings have spiritual routines, and the main one is entering complete into God's presence. Nobody escapes before the altar. It is necessary to be humble and responsible to deal with the dirt and it does no good to sweep it under the rug.

When people truly know each other, they end up learning both the defects and virtues of the other. The bad side of people doesn't surface in a superficial relationship.

Dysfunctional relationships are created due to a lack of proximity. It is not the Internet or the phone that separates or brings people together. We are the ones who decide to flee from reality or invest in the virtuousness of a superficial relationship in which the ashes and dirt are not seen.

In a superficial relationship, the dirt is there, but it is swept under the rug. Nobody wants others to know about their ashes, but they will appear sooner or later. What builds a relationship is routine, and marriage is routine. The dirt will inevitably appear sooner or later. Changing the routine does not resolve the problem; it only makes us more aware of our day-to-day. That which is different will be a welcome change when it proves harmonious with our routine. A good routine is about having healthy and constant habits. The novelty of life is always created within relationships and never outside them.

The person we marry is also the one who best knows our flaws. Every time we throw the ashes away, we create a dynamic for welcoming in the new. There is only one way to better get to know people, and that's by relating to them. In the beginning, everything is new. Nobody knows the bad stuff about the other. It's not considered important to reveal the dirt. But it's there and if it has not yet been seen, it means that the relationship is not yet complete.

The conflict is inherent to the relationship itself and fleeing from it does not resolve a relationship. The technology of the altar is not limited to pointing out errors; it also serves to point us in the right direction.

Parents and children create complex relationships as well. It makes no sense to allow our children to do whatever they want and make everything as comfortable as possible. If you make things easy, you don't discipline. You sweep the world's dirt under the rug. Comfort is imprisoning. That is why parents pay attention as to whether they are raising children or just growing bananas.

God also acts this way with us. Comfort weakens the dynamics of the relationship. It impedes life from becoming a journey in learning. He wants you whole! He wants to teach you and relate to you.

The worse kind of solitude is not about being close or far, single or married, alone or with someone. Rather, it is about being far from the destiny that God has planned for our lives. We only get closer to our destiny when we seek a relationship with God.

***

Our life should be one full of accomplishments, victories, and truths. It is easy to dream every night. The hard part is fighting for a dream. One only learns to fight by knowing how to dominate the adversary who ends up becoming our ally. Time is a favorable weapon and is not one pointed at our heads. We must take advantage of it. Of all the resources to which we have access, time is one of the most precious. It has a volatile and non-renewable nature. It is worth a lot, and that is why we must use it in our favor.

Thinking too much about the past and fantasizing too much about the future takes our focus off today, since it stops us from concentrating on life, which is the present. The clock cannot enslave us.

Lewis Carroll's celebrated classic *Alice in Wonderland* addresses this issue well. The book begins with a cute little girl, who after falling asleep while reading a book awakens frightened by the noise of an elegant white, fluffy rabbit wearing a vest and carrying a watch in his pocket. The valiant and hurried rabbit was visibly stressed and had a tense look in his eye. Looking at his watch constantly, he insistently repeated: *I'm late! I'm late!*

Always late for some event, he lived under intense pressure. Alice becomes intrigued and follows the rabbit. She follows it to a burrow, which is actually a tunnel that leads her to Wonderland. Following an uncertain path, she finds exotic creatures along the way. The rabbit's future was defined by an unorganized present; it was enslaved by time, suffocated by routine and commitments. Later, Alice meets another strange character, the Mad Hatter. This character was a man who fought against time; he believed that the clock had stopped at six o'clock in the afternoon and that, therefore, it was always teatime. Unlike the white rabbit, the Mad Hatter lived in the present and experienced each passing moment in a carefree manner and without any concerns. Holding on to a teapot made from fine porcelain, he was singing, laughing, and celebrating with his friends when Alice appeared. She interrupted the event and apologized for having invaded the birthday tea party.

The Mad Hatter laughed and said that it was not a birthday, but rather an "unbirthday." For him, today was the priority. In his opinion, there was only one day during the year in which you celebrate your birthday. Therefore, the other 364 days are "unbirthdays" and those days are special and unique too!

The Mad Hatter's watch did not work right, but his calculations were clever. He calculated happiness based on the "unbirthdays," and, therefore, his happiness was much greater. Actually, it was 365 times greater than the rabbit's. The Mad Hatter had complete control over time; time was his friend.

Alice learned two paths. That of the white rabbit, who saw the watch as his master, almost like a gun pointed at his head. And then there was the way of the pleasant time, the tamed and gentle watch, which allowed the Mad Hatter to live a *CARPE DIEM* life, to live every moment as it is unique and exclusive.

How can a balance be found between the white rabbit and Mad Hatter? One enslaved by time, and the other spurning the mechanics of time. All of us experience this dilemma. I myself have heard many times the phrase "life begins at 40," but when we are 21, we think that this will take an eternity to happen. However, time flies, and when we reach this age, certain questions are inevitable.

Reflecting on the past always awakens regret. And the past, what about it? Is it over? I am 100% convinced that it is possible to change the past. That is right! You did not read wrong. I insist; it is possible to change the past! However, the first thought that comes to mind is that the past is static and unalterable, that we create the present now; and the future is dynamic, a consequence of the present. So what magic is this?

What I want to say is not as absurd as it seems. We will change the past, but let us do it in parts. Could it be that the past is so cruel to us? Could it be that we do not learn absolutely anything from it? If it served absolutely nothing to you, then you were not a good student and did not learn the lesson! But do not blame yourself too much; you can change it now. The past changes! Yes, the past changes! And if it changes, your present also changes, and consequently your future will also change.

The perception of the past that we have today is different from the perception of the past we had yesterday. The perception of the past that we had six months ago is different than the perception of the past that we had two years ago. As we begin to draw away from the events of our life, or in other words, as we travel along the time line, our perception changes. A look at the past becomes less tragic and vivid in our memory. If you look at it intentionally, not with eyes of misfortune, tragedy, sadness, and conformism, but with eyes of complacence and wisdom of those who have a clear notion that they must thirst for change, then you will be automatically readjusting your past and rewriting the history of your life based on your interests and needs. This is the fruit of a maturity that must be cultivated, since everything in life requires technique and methodology. Understand that everything is a matter of perspective. Sometimes, a tragedy is similar to the collapse of a home, as if the pillars that sustained your life cracked and imploded. And when a collapse like this occurs, a gigantic cloud of dust and smoke rises into the air, irritating your eyes. Some personal tragedies in our lives cause the same effect. You become suffocated, you cannot breath well, and the problems in your life disorient you to the point that it is hard to find the way out from the middle of the wreckage.

Changing the past, however, is the key to the time machine. Adopt a different perspective and analyze the period, circumstances, options, fears, and truths. Yes, there were other possibilities, but the “ME” of the past is not the “ME” of the present. Be benevolent to yourself. Learning is the good inheritance of past errors. Hold on to this inheritance and not to the wreckage. This makes a huge difference.

By embarking on a journey into the past, you change the future. You become the master of time. Be the owner of it, not the slave. Plan, rethink, and do it now. Do not leave it for later. Do not wait, since today is to be lived. Today may be the D-Day of our lives. The day to recognize the importance of a true God and stop throwing words away into the wind; worshiping our ego, our vanity, our weaknesses, and primarily, our desperation. The smoke disappears, the dust settles, the road becomes more visible, and it is your job to continue along the journey.

Understanding success means undergoing an inner transformation. The word enthusiasm comes from the Greek word ENTHEOS: EN = Inside, THEOS = God, which means,

"To be full of God", to have God within us. The Greeks were polytheistic, meaning that they believed in several gods. Therefore, an enthusiastic person was one possessed by one of the gods, and because of this, he or she could transform nature and make certain things happen.

An enthusiastic person is one who believes in their capacity to transform things, to make things right. Enthusiastic is the person who believes in him or herself and believes in other people. He or she believes that people must transform the world and transform their own reality.

There is only one way to be enthusiastic: by acting enthusiastically! If we previously define a series of premises and conditions that we consider to be ideal, we will never become enthusiastic about anything, since there will always be reasons to atrophy this feeling.

It is not success that generates enthusiasm; it is enthusiasm that brings success. Enthusiasm is magnetic. It attracts and absorbs opportunities, transforming them to our benefit. There are people who wait for conditions to get better, for life to get better, or for success to reach them and to later get enthusiastic. The truth is that these people will never become enthusiastic about anything. Enthusiasm is what brings a new vision of life. And this enthusiasm must necessarily be connected to the absolute belief in the shielding provided from the power and favor that comes from God.

Growing means believing; believing means having an attitude. Having an attitude means declaring victory and living this in advance. Accordingly, the instruction that comes from God changes our life. Faith is the point of contact with the Creator.

Despite all the mountains of difficulties that may exist in front of you at this moment, you still have a spark of faith. And it is precisely this that you must activate now.

If someone makes you feel inferior, this may occur because you yourself are letting them. If other people's opinions are more important than building your own self-esteem, then you need to reprogram your mind. You can change your history, provided that you use the right method. You can explore your potential to the maximum. The choice is yours; it does not depend on anyone else. There are no excuses.

We have to let go of emotions
that are harmful to us.

We cannot allow ourselves to engage in self-sabotage. We cannot let ourselves be dominated by disintegrating and destabilizing emotions. We must look to the power and favor from God and stay focused on constructive feelings. We must concentrate and meditate on the good qualities so that they multiply within us.

When people lament and grumble about the circumstances that God gives them, they are actually complaining about God. Our language must generate transformation. We have to reeducate our speech.

The reeducation of speech will require a transformation in our way of thinking and acting. This set of actions will give us the capacity to act and not just react like a punch-bag that receives a blow, swings back into place, and does not have any alternative but to get hit.

While we currently have blood flowing through our veins, it now is time to let globules of faith circulate in our blood, embracing and defending our organism. In a certain sense, God performs a check-up on us. In this new type of blood test, he knows the count of the faith globules we have. A low number of faith globules allow us to only react to problems. We live reacting without the strength to change. In order to activate our creative potential, we must act and not just react. Our body must change. Our blood must change; our faith must reach another level; our transformation must be profound and organic. Faith will run in our veins, and certainty will dominate us. Our minds will become sharp, astute, and vibrant and our creative potential will become a transforming reality.

A transforming reality is something that only happens through movement. Without movement, there is no transformation. Movement is the key to everything. Faith is the gymnastics of the spirit. Those who do not exercise it, lose their agility. We must "practice" faith like an athlete works on his physical conditioning. Faith must be strong, resistant and have a variety of movements with major amplitude. A sedentary and rusty person is mono-articulate.

Without movement, nothing happens. Moses knew this and entered the Red Sea without it having been parted yet. He got his legs wet and continued forward before the miracle. He moved.

We are the leaders of ourselves, since we have the capacity for movement, and things only happen when there is movement. Our movements are less flaccid and hesitant when the blood circulation is good. Our faith is the same: consistent, true, absolute, and organic. It is not occasional, it does not circulate irregularly as a circulatory spasm; it circulates on a large scale, with anti-bodies against dismay, uncertainty, doubt, and fear. Our faith is organic, latent, unlimited, and abundant. It produces movement. We generate transformation when the certainty that exists is organic, real, and full. That is why we are made of the same material as our dreams.

It is not height, weight, or muscles that make a person big. It is not the weight shown on the scale or the height shown on the measuring tape that indicates greatness and size. A person is a giant when, as well as seeking alternatives for his or her growth, he or she is also concerned with and participates in the dreams of the people around him or her. In the same way, a person is small when he or she avoids all the responsibility of interacting with others, paying attention only to his or her objectives.

A person is big when they forgive, understand, and puts themself into another person's shoes.

Moses lived a dream, a dream of freedom. He thought of something, seeking collective success. His dream was so good that everyone should have something like it. His dream was gigantic. It could have been cut up and distributed without losing its original strength.

Those who have a dream, have hope. We weave our life and sow our future with dreams, objectives, purposes, and desires. Take away a dream and you will kill a person. It will be their end.

If we do not believe in our dreams,
we run the risk of a personal suicide.

We are the size of our dreams. It is easy to dream when the refrigerator is full, the rent paid and with tickets for a week vacation in the Caribbean kept safe in the drawer. Believing in the daily manna is what's difficult. The act of dreaming, of tracing the lines of a brilliant future, the initiative to project the future with an empty refrigerator, with a negative bank account, indicates the size of our dreams and the material from which they are made. We are made of the same stuff as our dreams. If you really desire something, if your objective is something crucial for your life, then your body will be resistant and try with the same intensity as your dreams, since you are made of the same stuff as them.

The manna was a clear indication of restitution of provisions and supplies. The Hebrew people followed an order and, like a signal, received food on a daily basis. They spent 40 years in the desert without any shopping centers, without bottled sparkling water, without department stores to buy shoes and clothing. It is God who cares for his people when they are in the desert. And the people in the desert were prosperous. You reach a level of prosperity when restitution comes from God. Restitution is a signal that our difficulties and our deserts are coming to an end.

If the people had not been abandoned for 40 years, why should we not be? If your desert is currently reflected by a lack of credit at the bank, a lack of credit with friends and family, then you need restitution. Being restituted means once again having credit, without being judged based on the past, without interest or monetary correction.

In fact, the past gives us a false impression of having disappeared, of having been buried. Occasionally, however, it re-emerges from nowhere. It is as if it missed us as much as we miss it. When we least expect it, there it appears slyly, popping up in the strangest places. If we decide to go to the movies, we buy popcorn and a soft drink, sit down, and there comes the past! It sits down beside us, smiles, slaps our back, grabs for our popcorn, raises it to its mouth, eats it, swallows, burps, and says: BOO!

We become low-spirited, scared, but it remains completely indifferent. After having scared us, it gets up and leaves. If this past still scares us, it is because we have not changed. The fright increases proportionally to our belief that we are capable of resolving everything alone. Prosperity is not the result of brute force. And that is why many do not prosper. We have to know where to invest; if there is a return, then it is an investment. Otherwise, the expense is wasted. Many people want prosperity as a reward for their work. Prosperity is a signal of an alliance.

Those who prosper are the ones who build alliances with those who are prosperous. It is the result of obedience to the instruction that comes from God. A dream is the same as a child. It is a gestation. A dream guaranteed by the power and favor from God is the certainty of its fulfillment.

Being paid in the same currency as our dreams is something wonderful.

If the instruction from God talks about an abundant life, however, and if this dream was not torn from your hearing, then it may come true, because God takes pleasure in making us happy. And man takes pleasure in the things he does. Two factors separate dreams from reality. The first is the raw material of the dream. Its consistency cannot be made up of doubts and uncertainties. Its durability and lifecycle determine its existence and strength. The second factor is the obstacles in our way. When we expect God's favor, we can remove those obstacles from our path and nothing will stop them from coming true. But remember, the dream is made from the same stuff as our faith. If we are flaccid and diluted in our convictions, they will also be this way.

The instruction from God guarantees that we have the right to take joy in our achievements. The dream is an objective that precedes the execution of a project.

This was when I saw that the best thing for man is to take joy in the things he does. This is why man exists.

So fight. Go back to the trenches and battle it out with the heralds of pessimism, the prophets of chaos, the messengers of impossibilities, and the public relations of darkness. Return to the battle trench. Abandon pessimism; always fight for your objectives, since the failed man is not he who arrives last, but rather he who gives up in the middle. We are the fruits of a dream.

CHAPTER 4

UNLOCKING THE SACRED

Controversies are like sparks on a bare wire: if we touch them, we will certainly get a shock. It is always much easier to give others the responsibility for arguing, seeking to protect ourselves from any possible confrontations, since generally speaking arguments whose central theme is religion take us nowhere.

Religion transcends freethinking. It overpowers the critical conscience; it is untouchable and is always viewed as something taboo, primarily in these days where conflicts and clashes between civilizations are scientifically studied.

For these reasons, most people avoid the topic under the maxim that "religion is not to be discussed." This causes additional issues because many people are only able to think about God if this reflection is tied to a "religious system," like the so many that exist around the world.

It is extremely difficult to disassociate God from a structured religious system. It is precisely due to this difficulty that we stop accepting him, since it is so easy to confuse God with this system and since we intuitively believe that religion will somehow give God structure, shape, personality, and thinking, so much so that it seems that God is a product of religion that seeks to make him more real, more palpable, and as convincing as possible. This conclusion is completely wrong. God and religion are two entirely different things. Our capacity for perception is color-blind and has a hard time perceiving this difference.

Those who do not delve into this universe have the clear impression that these religious systems are prisons, dungeons of ignorance, and the people who inhabit them are victims of a contemporary inquisition sentenced to a painful torture that even reaches levels of sordidness.

Those who criticize the religious world believe this universe consists of people who have committed "intellectual suicide" and who should be immobilized in straightjackets, since this is the appropriate garment for those who come to have a series of strange and mentally ill behavior.

Could it be that religion is the alienation caused by the transplant of brains, which were surgically removed from the skull and thrown into buckets steeped in detergent, fabric softener, and bleach to rid them of all traces of their capacity to think? The fear of being brainwashed makes people defensive about the countless justifications to flee the inevitable contact with the creative and maintaining force of the universe: God.

However, there are also those who seek to find him. And they look for him in the strangest of places. They look in the garden, at the bus stop, at the beach, at the bakery, the bookstore, at home, sifting through drawers, turning over closets, and they even search as if it were all a big game of hide-and-seek.

When they finally find him, they experience a feeling involving both relief and indignation, with a cry that cannot be kept quiet.

That's just great! Where do you think you are going?
Are you trying to run away from me?

God hunting season did not begin today. From far in the ancient past man has always been looking for a superior being. He was looking for God long before the emergence of Internet search engines and the globalization of information. Most of these attempts ended up in religion, and religion is this:

> Man in search of God using his own efforts and methods, trying to classify and prepare this God based on his own system of rites, doctrines, and conventions.

Religion undoubtedly has a strong conservative structure and an authoritative and hierarchical organization to it. Renewal (and any change that may occur in this universe) will always constitute an uncertainty. That is why it is something not easily accepted by the religious structure.

In the past power was in the hands of the intermediate agents, the clerical elite, and powerful warriors and monarchs. Kings held power because they declared themselves to be the inheritors of a divine right. Their legitimacy could not be questioned. During that time the explanation for natural phenomena depended exclusively on the gods and the interpretation of those who represented them. The understanding of the world originated from the divine.

From there, man has slowly progressed towards a quest with some logical reason, which began to earn space for itself through the thinkers and philosophers who shaped public opinion, since these began to legislate and influence the societies in which they lived. Thought, however, is not static: it follows several different paths. When we go up a step, the only certainty that we have is that if we remain there, we will get nowhere, and that is what pushes us upward to the next level.

During this climb there also emerged a concern with explaining reality as something that could be proven with scientific reasoning. In a world with multiple realities and ways of thinking, the repudiation and intellectual denial of an entire reality built on the belief of a world created, organized, and maintained by God has also appeared.

Atheism is characterized by non-belief in the existence of gods. This absence generally comes from a deliberate philosophical decision or the difficulty in believing in religious teachings, which may seem literally "incredible." Atheists affirm that their lack of faith does not stem from a simple ignorance of religious teaching, but rather is a deliberate and conscious choice.

THE HEYDEY OF "HOMO-STUPIDUS"

The French philosopher Auguste Comte, the father and self-declared founder of sociology in the 18th century, explained society through positive reason. According to Comte, science was proven reason and philosophy was speculative reason. At that time it was perceived that there was a need for intellectual reform.

In order to understand the world, it was necessary to understand social structures, and, for Auguste Comte, the advancement of the individual ended up generating the advancement of social structures. Comte believed that humanity followed a trajectory that started with the theological phase, in which man depended on divinities to explain natural phenomena. Gods were required to understand the world. According to this perspective this phase was followed by the metaphysical phase, in which logical reason began to be developed by philosophers and thinkers. In this stage this type of reason predominated but it was still not scientific. Finally, Comte spoke of the positive phase, that of Positivism. For him, social science was capable of explaining society as a living and biological organism, since the human spirit, by recognizing the impossibility of obtaining absolute responses, gives up trying to seek the origin and destination of the universe and concentrates on systemizing the laws and behavioral standards of the world through reasoning and empirical observation. According to Comte, positive science should ensure the progress and construction of industrial society, but the new order would require a positive, scientific religion. Curiously, after so many essays and theories, Comte ended up creating a religion, the Positivist Church, in which the Great Being was socially adapted to the new society. This is because order implies hierarchy, and religion could be an important tool in the society idealized by Comte. Since he was a vehement critic of the theological and metaphysical state of some societies, he ended up serving as the device of a new religious idea that put the image of a woman on an altar (Clotilde de Vaux, his platonic passion). Comte's position leaves it clear that ambiguity in relation to religion affects all minds, from the most privileged to the most simple. Comte's influence was so important in Brazil that the motto found on the country's flag, "Order and Progress," is clearly Positivist, coming from Republicans who based their beliefs on these concepts.

***

What is interesting about Auguste Comte's line of thought is that he believed that theological society would evolve into a new positive order that would be the natural result of progress and technology. Recently, however, the contemporary philosopher John Gray, Professor of European Thought at the London School of Economics, stated that faith in progress is an illusion, since man does not control his destiny and for this reason scientific advances do not have any association with ethics. If science could be understood as a gradual way of understanding how God works in nature, Adam and Eve would have empirically understood the law of action and reaction long before Isaac Newton! It seems that the apple always plays a leading role in major discoveries—even though you do not believe me, I am not referring to Steve Jobs when I say such a thing.

If we think that the fruit of knowledge of good and evil, which was in the Garden of Eden and eaten by Adam and Eve, symbolizes knowledge, discretion, technology, and progress, we can see that it has given us serious indigestion, because our ethical problems are still far from being resolved by technology. On the other hand, if God had not given Adam and Eve the opportunity to choose, they could essentially be robots, simply doing what they were programmed to do. God created Adam and Eve to be "free" beings, capable of making decisions and choosing between good and evil. To ensure that they were truly "free," there had to have been a choice. However, we are not always sensible in our choices.

Religion is essentially a choice, a human alternative that brings comfort to some and power to others. Curiously enough, many religions are defined by and based on fear, primarily the fear of death. If there were no physical death, they would no longer have any power of persuasion and coercion over mankind. The religious system transforms the fear of death into a heavy chain, one that is tightly fastened around the neck with a padlock. Instead of offering the master key that relieves such fear, religious representatives replace old padlocks with stronger ones.

The religious recipe that brings false salvation needs an object God and that is why it searches for God, making him the target to be reached, gagged, and subjected to human needs and interests. The recipe works like this:

> First you look for God, next you classify him, and then you gag him. Finally, he is transformed into a mere supporting actor in a religious system belonging to a few clerics and theologians.

Within this perspective, God is not allowed to be God, God cannot be God, and that is why man "kills" God. Friedrich Wilhelm Nietzsche, the 19th century German philosopher, was not wrong when he said: *God is dead! God remains dead, and it was we who killed him!*

He is dead for those who live absorbed by the world of religion and its forms of power. They in fact, are who killed him. However, he did not die; he obviously survives. And if he survives, how can we allow living corpses to call themselves his representatives? In what notary office, in what jurisdiction, and at what moment in the history of humanity did God grant some power-of-attorney to these representatives?

I dare say, without fear of error, that God's proposal was never to make us religious, but rather to bring us nearer and give us a level of intimacy with him, which would give us a life full of benefits and bounty in all areas.

The existence of religion and all forms of worship, even in the most distinct civilizations, peoples, and cultures, only serves to show us just how much the concept of eternity and thirst for spirituality are engraved in the human heart. It is as if our genome carried within it a characteristic inherent in the "Adamic" species that leads us to seek the divine. More simply put, it is part of our essence and our nature.

The very nature of religion is conservative, exclusivist, and dogmatic, and like a great living organism, it erects walls and barriers, separating people and reconstructing the borders of new identities.

Spirituality, however, converges into union. Religion divides, spirituality unites.

Although religion may subliminally profess this, God is not the property of any one group. He is not the trademark of any organization. He does not belong to any traditional or contemporary institution. God is God and as God, he is free and sovereign. He cannot be manipulated; he reveals himself to whomever he wants, when he wants, how he wants, where he wants, and does not ask permission or say sorry to anyone in particular.

When we turn back the hands of the clock and take a look into the past, looking through old records and events, we inevitably become perplexed, observing how much wrong people have done to their brothers, discriminating and humiliating one another in the name of religious faith.

Religious faith greatly surpasses the faith that originated in the quest for spirituality. Faith in religion generated religious structure, which in turn generated social organization.

We live in a world generated by religious faith. Within this perspective, one may hastily conclude that religion is disastrous or at least a necessary evil, but this conclusion is far too simplistic and superficial, since it neither observes nor respects the individuality of personal contact with faith that generates religion.

There is a very fine line between criticism of the religious system and being enforcers of other faiths. The risk of being disrespectful to what is sacred may transform us into exactly that which we do not want to be: intolerant beings.

We cannot desensitize ourselves to the world of the sacred. We do not have this right, much less this prerogative, since we do not come with a built-in spiritual X-ray that reveals to us the ways and paths of anyone's heart.

Speaking of the world of the sacred, the greatest distinction between religions, from the perspective of their formats and practices, is basically the weight given to what is sacred and what is profane.

It is in this battle between the sacred and the profane where values and rituals are located. The sociologist Emile Durkheim was one of the first to address this issue. The characteristics of the sacred world make people more introspective and restrained. The separation between the profane and the sacred appears even in our gestures. We are more silent, more respectful, more reverent, and less extravagant; we speak more softly, we lower our head in respect, and we are more restrained when faced with something perceived as sacred. Rituals intensify values and act as catalysts of faith. They represent the instrumental faith. Faith in action involves rituals and, even without the weight of religion, our lives are entirely ritualized.

It is obvious that no one lives without traditions and conventions. They are a necessity of life. Civil and legislative codes include countless examples. Law is an instrument of power—containing rules, laws, and limits—and it is not written to preserve what is just, but rather tries to be guided by what is right. Law is reactive, not causal. The main characteristic of Anglo-Saxon law is that it is based on customs and traditions, in other words, common sense.

We live immersed in traditions and do not even realize this. We only stop the car when traffic lights are red due to a convention guaranteed by law. In many urban centers and in certain neighborhoods and vicinities, this convention has already been "abolished" after 11:00 p.m. due to safety reasons. There are few police officers who would punish us for this crime. They, more than anyone, are aware that the most sensible measure in these cases is to go against the code.

Fashion is a typical example of aesthetic conventions based on a tradition that continually renews and updates itself dynamically. If certain women buy platform heels and bell-bottom jeans, they are using a temporary style, in other words, something that reflects current fads.

A few years ago the same clothes would have been regarded as so inelegant and incompatible with the reality of the time that people would have avoided dressing that way out of fear of being ridiculed. If we go even further back in time we could certainly find some place in the not so distant past where this style would appear new and exciting. Dynamics require changes that often involve going back, going in the opposite direction, or are in opposition to current trends.

The religious phenomenon cannot simply be viewed as a world that exists solely in the imagination of certain people who follow creative and influential leaders skilled at producing symbols and rules. Symbols and conventions involve screening beliefs, and are the result of sensory and empirical experiences based on a book that codifies the faith. All this generates a tradition.

The religious base of Western civilization is predominantly constructed on top of and linked to the Judeo-Christian culture and, therefore, uses what is almost the same book of faith, although with entirely different approaches and interpretations. The common denominator is what is called in Hebrew the *Tanakh*, known in the Christian world as the Old Testament.

In the *Tanakh* a piece of clothing used in Jewish religious practices is mentioned, which serves as an example of an interesting case of sacralization. Essentially the *tallit* is a rectangular piece of cloth used as a prayer shawl by Jews in their morning religious ritual. Its four corners have fringes with a series of knots called *tzit-tzit*. These fringes symbolize the commandments of the Torah (the Pentateuch, also known as the five books of Moses, part of the *Tanakh*).

The *tallit* expresses the idea of covering the spirit in sanctity to fulfill divine laws and to remember that we should not follow the evil impulses of our hearts, in addition to reinforcing a concept of equality and of the non-differentiation of men before God.

Orthodox Jews wear the *tallit* routinely, and not just at synagogues or during prayer. This ritual is sacred for them, since it establishes a daily pattern of respect for God's commandments. This commandment is found in the book that serves as the common denominator between the Jewish and Christian cultures, but it is not regarded as a relevant commandment in Christianity, despite its wide-ranging multi-denominational nature.

Yeshua, who was born and raised as a Jew, would have followed this commandment in an Orthodox fashion, something that, until the present, was an exclusively Jewish practice. For him, the *tzit-tzit* did not only have a ceremonial function, but also represented his zeal for the instruction from God and his respect for the sacred.

There is an extremely interesting passage about a hemorrhagic woman who touched the fringes of Jesus' clothes (which were actually his *tzit-tzit*).

Jesus was frequently in the middle of a crowd. It was inevitable that the presence of the rabbi Yeshua (his name in Hebrew) would attract crowds, even if the majority of the people who sought him did not get the opportunity for personal contact. Many followed him simply out of curiosity. He was a well-known figure at the time, on the periphery of the Roman Empire, in a region of little importance within the nation of Israel. If there had been paparazzi two thousand years ago, they would have certainly followed his every step every day. However, it is important to note that, even when surrounded by thousands of people, he recognized that someone touched him in the middle of a pressing crowd.

In the middle of the crowd that surrounded Jesus, a woman touched his clothing. This did not go unnoticed, since he asked: ***Who touched my tzit-tzit?***

He noticed that a woman touched his clothing. In an essentially patriarchal culture, the presence of a woman in itself was an act of courage. But there was also the touch. A hemorrhagic woman who sought the cure for a disease that had plagued her for twelve years. This must have been a time of disillusions and frustrated hopes for her, which certainly led her to cry many tears during sleepless nights and suffer terribly.

She probably had spent every penny she had on doctors. She was a fighter who tirelessly searched for a way to save her own life. Her disease was chronic and serious. Medicine offered no answers for her case. The physicians of the time could not help her. That woman was losing blood daily. Logic leads us to conclude that she had a serious type of anemia, making her so weak that she even found it hard to move around.

The hemorrhagic woman faced segregation due to her illness. She faced segregation in her married life, since a woman who bled constantly could not have relations with her husband. A menstruating woman was *niddah* ("impure" in Hebrew) and was prohibited from having sexual relations.

This woman was treated almost as if she had a contagious disease. She lived tormented by shame, with her self-esteem completely destroyed. That is why she anonymously came to touch Yeshua, with fear of being rejected, since anyone who had any contact with her would become ceremonially impure. The woman who had touched his *tzit-tzit* intentionally, and with a great deal of boldness, said:

If I only touch his tallit, I will be cured

She not only said that she would be cured if she touched that Hebrew garment, but she actually did touch it and was cured.

If her disease was an insurmountable wall, the sacred worked as a hammer that broke through the seal of impossibility. She recognized the sacredness of the object and was in turn supported by the scriptural base of faith that she professed. However, what transformed her life was her realization that what was described as sacred was capable of channeling the power to cure and regenerate. She did not use the sacred object as an amulet or bestow her faith in the object itself; she simply understood the practice of the relationship with the power and favor from God through faith. This case leaves room for much discussion: does the woman represent someone who lives for religion or someone who lives through religion?

After all, can religion be discussed?

The problem is not religion. The problem is living for religion as a purpose that is sufficient in itself. When religion becomes a fad, the objective and essence of life ends up gradually poisoning man and separating him from his initial purpose. On the other hand, in order for religion to survive, it must organize and adjust itself. That is why it becomes bureaucratic, hierarchical, and structurally dependent on administrative and legislative processes, unquestionably becoming a political organism. All of this structure creates expenses and costs and requires dedication and procedures, since it must interact with users, maintain relations with the authorities, and it must have an interpretation of the world. In order to structure a religious denomination, it is also necessary to be aware of peers and competitors.

This gives us a space for reflection, and allows us to think that there are many who surround Yeshua but who do not touch him through faith. There are countless people who practice religion but who do not perceive the dimension and effectiveness of the relationship with God. God is not only relationship-oriented, God is a relationship in a unique and fundamental way. An intimate relationship with God can only be built through effective communication. Only through Yeshua can you establish and re-establish an effective communication with God, and that's why we must pay careful attention to his words.

Yeshua never condemned rabbinic traditions. He condemned practices that supplanted God's will; he prioritized the word of God and valorized the essence.

Tradition saves no one. However, one cannot, under any hypothesis, confuse tradition with additions. Tradition can be better understood as a dimension of life that includes a scriptural base and religious conventions. Tradition is a set of ways of thinking; of doing or acting that leave such strong impressions in the past that they continue to have repercussions today. This is extremely important, since it is customs and traditions that create social order.

Modern culture originated in a morality that was initially linked to religion and then to ethics that absorbed religious customs and conventions. These conventions are religious practices that do not depend on a denominational core and may be associated with Judaism, Methodism, Presbyterianism, Lutheranism, Pentecostalism, Catholicism, Positivism, with "isms" in general, and primarily with the largest existing denomination, which is "Ialoneism."

Interestingly, Christianity is a multi-denominational religious concept based on the Messianic figure Yeshua, but it is not a religious culture based essentially on the religion that he practiced.

What is culture? Culture is a vast word. In the 20th century, one of the world's most influential men in the area of education was Paulo Freire—a Brazilian who once defined culture through a very unique phrase: *Milk is nature and cheese is culture.* In other words, he stated that culture is also the transformation of nature. Food is a product of culture. That is why we talk about Chinese food, Mexican food, and Italian food.

In fact, milk is the world's most highly consumed food. Milk produces cheeses, yogurts, ice creams, butter, etc. Second place goes to wheat—the main raw material used in breads and edible dough.

Taste cannot be discussed, but observe that coincidentally, Yeshua's first miracle was to transform water into wine. Actually, the meaning of the idiomatic expression about transforming water into wine means transforming something bad into something wonderful. The transformation of water into wine is a metaphor as well for a cultural action. Wine does not sprout from nature. It needs to be made. It is a by-product of grapes, water, and man's work. It depends not only on being present in nature, but also on man's transforming action.

And the wine used by Yeshua ritualistically during the Passover, could it be something cultural? From what culture? The local or universal one? Hebrew, Chinese, Mexican, or Italian?

If it were simply some content of a local culture, anyone would be free to celebrate Passover or the Lord's Supper with the most popular drink from his or her own country. I myself would do it with an aromatic and flavorful coffee. However, in doing so, I would most certainly generate some controversy because wine is not a mere component of the local culture, since it became a very part of the culture of religion.

So, religion is culture. If you were not a part of your culture, you would be a secularized individual.

That is why Paul of Tarsus talks about the existence of a god of this century. Every time he refers to this god, he is also referring to a secularized culture, which is one that exists outside the values of the biblical message.

And counterculture? The culture of contesting, which is the alternative to the dominant culture. So, religion can be culture and at the same time counterculture.

It is not possible to live without belonging to a social group or without sharing a certain vision of the world based on values, norms, and language.

It doesn't mean that the culture is either good or bad; it means that the values are different. In the same sense, it cannot be stated that one culture is better than another, just like it cannot be said that Chinese food is better than Mexican food.

Yeshua's message is a culturally Jewish one, but one which transcends local culture because it is at the same time universal.

The expression "religious syncretism" talks about a miscegenation of religions. In the etymological sense of the word, syncretism means "united front of the Cretans," symbolizing the joint agreement that the citizens of Crete formed against their common enemy. Later, this word came to mean the merger between opposing tendencies, primarily during a period in which religious conflicts predominated.

Every time that some religion or faith absorbs the elements of another, it is characterized as syncretism. However, this phenomenon may appear in a less subtle manner, since there is no 100% pure faith, since all of us blend secular values with those of biblical morality.

Our syncretism is cultural because we blend values and create a faith that is customized to fit our interests.

The transformation of water into wine is also a metaphor for transformation beyond the cultural aspect, since what is implicit is the transformation of human character. However, syncretism blends and transforms Yeshua's word to fit secular values. Take a look at this new gospel below:

> Well ventured is the man who has many dollars.
> Well ventured is the man who travels first class.
> Well ventured is the man who is powerful and famous.

Marketing always seeks to always sell us what we lack.

This twisted gospel is a marketing strategy that opens our appetite for fame, money, and power. Prosperity is a consequence of the course taken and never the objective. God's word is the reflection of his character, thereby making it an invitation to live in harmony with God himself. A good wine is perfect for toasting the victory of the transformation of secular values into the values of God's character.

***

Yeshua's thought and practice reflected an ancient, unique, and special wisdom. He was a walking encyclopedia who knew the words and more than anyone else was able to transmit the essence of every lesson. The prayer *Shema Israel,* which is the essence of Judaism, was emphatically cited by him, something that is easy to notice even in a superficial reading of the gospels. In the wide range of translations, it is very clear that he taught, mentioned, and referred to *Shema Israel* as the maximum expression of God's love. But why is this important? What is the point?

The recognition of God's sovereignty is fundamental, since it can be understood as his authority, dominion, and absolute rule over all known reality. Yeshua said this and emphasized that together with the principal of *Shema Israel*, love for others was fundamental and that these two instructions constituted the backbone of God's commands.

These aspects provide the basis for all teachings from God. They are the key of this chapter and the most significant foundation of all the complications of divine teaching. By reiterating and confirming this instruction from the Book of Deuteronomy, Yeshua eliminates all doubts and leaves it clear that the main commandment is:

Hear O Israel, the Lord is our God, the Lord is one.

Regardless of whether we fully or partially agree, if we accept it with no restrictions or in a fragmented fashion, whether we deal with it light-heartedly or seriously, the importance of this statement remains the same. It is an immutable truth, an irrefutable truth. If we look to the side, to the left, to the right, if we look up, look down, or in any direction, the sovereignty and existence of God are unalterable facts, even if they are displeasing to some. And the fact that God is one leaves no space for two, three, or four. It leaves no space for multiple colors, shades, tones, grades, or variations.

This is the basic premise of all the instruction that benefits us. The fact that Yeshua recognizes, reiterates, and reaffirms this categorically underscores and strengthens this instruction because he was most responsible for revealing the profundity of the interpretation of each word of God. Of all his teachings, this is the main one. His discourse was democratic and inclusive, preaching that the truth had to be told. He fled from religious exclusivity.

This truth could not be kept hidden, restricted to a select public. This truth was universal. That is why he touched even those excluded by the social, political, and religious hierarchy of his time.

Prejudice is not a problem confined to a certain period or region. It is a problem found in different centuries and generations. Yeshua felt no prejudice. So much so that he shared his table with tax collectors, a hated category at the time since they worked for the then dominating and invasive foreigner. Yeshua also shared his table with prostitutes and thieves, the underworld of his time. His attitude pointed towards the transforming character of the truth, a message of regeneration that dispensed with privilege and hierarchy.

If we could compare prejudice to a contagious bacterium, we would observe that it grows in the furnace of misery. Prejudice, however, is not natural. Nobody is born with a gene telling them to hate what is different. Rather, prejudice is the product of a historical and social process constructed over time. It has no logical base. In a world where the state creates or allows the creation of prosperity, neither the extreme right nor the extreme left would be able to increase their number of activists and militants. If misery increases, the state decreases, political extremism increases and religion expands its influence. They exclude rebels because they want economic and social opportunities. If the oppressed and excluded had the cultural condition to create a small organization, the glasshouse would be much bigger. In today's world, many of the excluded, to whom only minimum citizenship is offered, have globalized their revolt, crossing borders or have become involved in organized crime, political activism, or religious fundamentalism.

Yeshua taught forgiveness, tolerance, respect, mercy, peace, and the importance of valuing life. Ironically, many atrocities have been committed in his name, including the Crusades and the Inquisition, even though he was a complete pacifist, an icon of tolerance, of inner and outer peace, the true peace that overcomes all real understanding. Why was he to blame if certain individuals unjustly used his name and his message and perverted the truth?

CHAPTER 5

Unlocking Negotiations

No father likes to see his child living in a messy room. Dealing with our adolescent children is always a major challenge, since they always see the person in control as a tyrant and the one being controlled is always the victim.

The victimization is always an excuse to avoid dealing with the mess, since acting this way shifts the focus. The victim does not question the disorder in his life, but rather chooses to focus on the commander's discernment in terms of wanting to lead his life.

Sometimes we are parents, and sometimes we are children. While we play the role of parents, we know that the problem of the mess is the collateral effect of a sickness called confusion. The confusion is not restricted to making a mess in the room alone, but also extends to all areas, such as studies, relationships, and health.

However, we are also children and the symptoms that afflict our children are the same ones that affect us. That which most bothers us about them is hard to diagnose in ourselves. The world is governed by order. Even if we cannot see the logic behind a succession of events, nothing in the universe happens by accident.

God is not the god of confusion. When our lives are nothing more than confusion, we are not living through God's will but rather our own. Confusion is tiring. It works like an energy drain that leads to exhaustion. To fight back against the fatigue, you need to choose the right medicine. However, it will not be based on food supplements, pills, or vitamins. We need to seek unity with God's principles.

We have a hard time understanding unity because we have a hard time understanding purpose. Unity is the purpose that leads us to common interest.

We were created for unity. What is the purpose of a marriage if there is no unity? What is the purpose of a congregation if there is no unity? What is the purpose of a company if the employees don't understand the corporation's vision and mission?

We need to reach an agreement with God. Most certainly, unity is the key to success in our material and spiritual life. Without a unity with God, we will be worshiping our internal idols, which generates confusion. It is not a theological issue, but rather about freedom from exhaustion.

The premise for unity is the development of a relationship. God's favor is not obtained at a bargaining table.

Negotiation is present in the lives of all human beings. From very early on, we learn to negotiate with our parents, using tears as the currency of exchange.

When we grow up, we learn to negotiate with suppliers and clients. Bargaining is associated with discounts, deadlines, and conditions. These elements are called "positions" and are all taken into consideration by those negotiations.

However, the negotiation is supported by the business interest as opposed to by the positions. Human beings are constantly bargaining. Even with God, when they make promises in exchange for a solution to their problems. The error made by the "homo-stupidus" is sitting at the bargaining table with God.

You cannot bargain deadlines, values, and conditions with God. That's why people are so exhausted. The confusion begins precisely there. God doesn't care about our "positions." We want to negotiate and he wants to build a relationship. The interests are different.

In primitive societies, the flow of goods and services took place through bartering, what defined commerce was the exchange of one piece of merchandise for another.

It was a simple process. Objects were exchanged in the same way as they are today, just as children intuitively exchange stickers at schools. A banana was traded for an apple, a piece of meat for a certain quantity of wheat. The exchanges were normally just, since they met the needs of both parties.

The world evolved, it needed to evolve and so did commerce. That is why in the following stage we find coins whose value was defined by weight and the purity of the precious metal. Accordingly, merchandise was parameterized and its value attributed to the equivalent in coins. Money is thus an instrument used to facilitate trade. Merchants, adepts of free trade used it to establish their rules and conventions, known as *Lex Mercatoria*, or the "Law of Merchants." This was not written anywhere, but it was fulfilled by all the ethical merchants, sometimes made official with a simple handshake.

The emergence of national states brought about the currency coined in gold or silver and then paper money, which was based on a precious metal, usually gold. Later, the gold standard was abandoned and the issuing of the money became free, based on the criteria of each monetary authority.

There is a type of unjust trade that despite harming one party, benefits the other in an exponential manner. It is an unthinkable trade, in which one of the sides voluntarily proposes to lose to the benefit of the other, who gains much more.

This exchange, which is represented through Yeshua carrying the burden of humanity and which goes against the logic of *Lex Mercatoria*, provides us with the solution to countless problems and torments. We will change when we submit to Yeshua. Even if circumstances do not change, if we change because of them, the final result will be positive.

This unfair trade that we make with Yeshua is what I call the REST FACTOR.

Look at the terms of this contract:

> ***Take my yoke upon you and learn from me, for I am gentle and humble in heart, and you will find rest for your souls. For my yoke is easy and my burden is light.***

This is the REST FACTOR, the problem solver that comes from God. However, at whom is this discussion directed? Could it be that there is a target audience? A defined public?

Yes, there is a target. The target is all of those who struggle and are overburdened. And who is overburdened? Well, if we live on planet Earth, then we will certainly have our afflictions and no lack of problems. This is because in the journey of life, it is natural for us to make new friends and enemies and create new problems. Could it be that we have at some moment given someone everything we have and received in exchange the worst of that other party? The pain was so bad that it bothers us even today? We try not to hold on to such hurts, but the bitter taste that got trapped in our throats still comes back every once in a while, bringing with it anger, the feeling that we would most certainly rather never feel, all of which creates a deep disappointment.

The worst deceptions, those that leave us marked until the end of our days, are those we thought were our friends.

Life's routine is defined by our free will; everything collaborates, helping us become more experienced in every way. The bruises hurt, we become less trusting, and this will probably create a defense mechanism that often makes us less friendly and pleasant. After all, does concern help anyone? If the answer is no, then we must dominate it.

When we are overburdened, logic indicates that if this symptom persists, it is because we are not putting into practice one of the most important commandments of the entire manual from God.

If we are not able to lay our head on the pillow and fall into a peaceful deep sleep—known as the "sleep of the just"—then it is possible that we have not achieved the necessary level of faith.

This occurs because we do not live what we have dreamed, what we profess, or what we believe.

If we do not believe that we can avoid our problems and dominate them with favor and power from God, we are living yet another bluff.

It is extremely difficult for us to disengage ourselves from our problems. This level of abstraction from reality can only occur by constructing a new reality based on something concrete, tested, and approved.

Trusting entirely in the REST FACTOR means saying that we are "shielded" like an armored car that transports money, where bullets and attacks do not penetrate the armor. If the armor is weak, the problems come back because we tie them to us with an invisible rope and pull them near us at various times. We are not able to move ourselves away from them and we live in function of them. In this way, our religion is concern, and our blessings are the collateral effects resulting from this stress.

The only thing missing is for us to make offerings and head out on processions to the great holy temple known as the pharmacy, where the pharmacist/priest reiterates and liturgically confirms our faith by giving us a miracle pill that is handed out to the devout of this religion, symbolizing our dependence and communion.

Nonetheless, all of us are really the people at whom Yeshua's teachings were directed, since if we struggle and are continuously struggling for survival, if we are fighting for our dreams, to become better people, fighting to believe in our authority, and to learn to exercise it, then this discussion is applicable to our lives. On the day we become leaders of ourselves, we will become the leaders of many. If this discussion is understood as objectivity and pragmatism, if it is taken literally, then the unfavorable circumstances of our lives will be seen in such a different light that it will bring about an enormous transformation in the course of our existence. Even if the circumstances do not change, our view of these obstacles will be so different that our reality will change. Through our gaze we will transmit truth, confidence, and serenity without the help of tranquilizers or any of those medications found on the shelves of pharmacies, since problems will no longer paralyze us.

A large number of people hibernate like bears inside a cave, waiting for winter to pass. Winter, however, is long, cold, and grey, and those who try to imitate bears seem to be increasingly cornered and afraid. The winter will only end when we gain the posture and humility to hear the wake up call.

The great truth is that we store the weapons
we have in the closet, lock it with a padlock,
and throw away the key.

If the authority and dominion bestowed upon us from God could be materialized through a deep mental exercise, in such a way that this authority and dominion assumed the shape of a cane, it would probably be locked away in the closet so it would not be able to scare the flies away. Our soul is tormented by the weight of our errors, and these errors make us feel an unsettling sensation of guilt. Nothing gives us peace, neither tranquility nor freedom. Our efforts to push God away and our inclination to do everything the wrong way contribute heavily to us carrying a tremendous weight in our hearts, which we carry with us as a kind of self-inflicted wound, since there is nothing that forces us to do so. We are heavily weighed down, because we guide our actions based on our own will in a "self-help" process.

There is a carefully planned strategy that allows us to attain the results of a more lighthearted and less disturbed life. God gave Yeshua the mission of solving problems to help us lift this burden off ourselves.

He is the agent of change. Every application of knowledge, tools, and skills available to us must pass through him. In this flowchart from ABOVE (heaven), there is no other way to obtain results, since there is no alternative that allows us to ignore the REST FACTOR.

It is finally time for us to understand our being, to identify our anxiety and anguish in order to have a clear perception that we need to rest. Our most immediate need is to have a different perspective of the circumstances.

Anxiety is a mental state generated within us. We have the expectation that something will happens in our favor. When this expectation is not fulfilled, anxiety—which is a dangerous sentiment—may emerge and become something much more serious, transforming itself into anguish. This anguish can, in certain cases, actually lead to stress, depression, and death. It is something very serious and should be handled with due attention.

Concern is the generating fact for this entire process and it is always associated with the future. It may be over the short or long term, since it does not always refer to distant times, but rather a moment that is quite close, sometimes the next moment. When tomorrow comes, today will already be over. Nonetheless, there is a promise. The promise is this:

I shall give you rest.

Consequently, we will find rest. If routine is tiring us out, and tiring out those who accompany us, if we are complaining too much, then it is not a vacation that we need; perhaps we simply need faith.

Yeshua did not address only those who felt just and dignified. He did not waste much time with the proud, with the ostensive, patrolling of those who only want to scorn values different from their own. He was extremely practical, directing his teachings to all those who labor and are overburdened.

Do you fit into this group? Bingo! Eureka! Then he was speaking precisely to you! This opens up new perspectives.

What an amazing difference it makes when we can see that there is an interaction, in which we are the main characters,

This is a transforming perception; it is pragmatic and practical. We can fly higher.

The story of Daedalus and Icarus is a well-known legend. Imprisoned on the Island of Minos, Daedalus builds wings made of feathers and wax for himself and for his son Icarus. However, Icarus got too close to the sun, and the wax that held together the feathers of his wings melted, causing him to fall into the sea and die.

The legend was a warning about the temptations to reach the sky, making it similar to the story of the Tower of Babel and exemplifying man's ancient desire to fly, trying to equal himself to God. The man who trusts the strength of his own arm, but who seeks help in himself, the "self-help" man, or "homo-stupidus" wants to fly using his own resources. He wants to use his attributes, such as: intelligence, logic, competition, creativity, and the wealth of resources, but lacks the essential ingredients that allow him to a achieve a sublime, peaceful flight without turbulence, without strikes by airline companies or air traffic controllers, a flight like that of the eagle.

Most people are not even able to take off, but remain on the ground. The anxiety of the world paralyzes us, makes us heavy, and loads us down with excess baggage. This excess robs us of our capacity to react. We only think about what we lack and what cannot be done.

Excess baggage is expensive, and if we do not rid ourselves of it, we will remain there taxiing on the runway, unable to fly.

When all of these hindrances are out of the way, we get some good news. We need the airport control tower to authorize the flight, for the runway to be cleared, and the baggage space immediately emptied. Excess baggage even negatively affects our life in the professional and corporate world. The capacity to discard and summarize is worth gold. North American writer Mark Twain responded to a friend who complained about the enormous length of one of his letters:

> ***I am sorry, I did not have time to write a short letter, that is why it was long.***

If even the words that we speak and write must be chosen carefully in order to guarantee that they are founded in objectivity, imagine the extra weight of our lives, containing thoughts of anxiety, fear, and anguish? Objectivity and efficiency require us to be selective and discard and suppress this extra weight.

To take off, however, there is something better. *Bessorah* is the Hebrew term corresponding to good news, or in other words the flight authorization. And good news is always welcome. It is new in the sense that it is revealed individually and chronologically at different moments during our personal journeys. It means that the Creator is near to man, and therefore, God is within our reach. It is time to reach out our hand, applying the REST FACTOR to our lives.

Could it be possible that human forces receive this kingdom, or authorization, without being instructed by the control tower?

Even if man has discipline and attitude, is obstinate, focused, and dedicated, he may not always find the strength in himself to remain loyal to the principal given by God.

We need extra strength to react since ours is not sufficient. We need to change from an occasional relationship with God to another one that is built upon a permanent commitment. After all, this occasional relationship, this flirting, is similar to an ad placed in the free classified section in a trade newspaper since it is not taken seriously; it is not dense and does not bring lasting perspectives.

To use an object, we must always ask permission from the owner. After borrowing something, anyone with a minimum sense of politeness will thank the person who loaned it to him or her. In the same way, when we want to use something that exists in the universe, we must ask permission from the Creator and the maintainer of the world. God gave us the permission to use and enjoy all of his creation and we have to know how to do it with respect and care, because the permission granted to us is not unconditional.

Knowing how to be thankful is fundamental.

***

Is it that we really understand this message?

There are conceptual models that try to explain the human communication process. It is actually not that complex—there is the sender, the message, and the recipient. For a company, it works similarly to a dialogue between two people.

In this case, the sender is the brand (company), which wants to communicate a message to the recipient (consumer). This message may be transmitted via some type of media (billboard, magazine, digital media, television, etc.) to the consumer.

One of the things I learned during my life is that when the recipient (consumer) does not understand the message, the "blame" falls to the sender, which failed to communicate correctly.

That is why it is important to know the target public with which we wish to communicate: so that we can ensure that it understands the message.

Can dogs talk? Perhaps not in human language, but they are capable of communicating. I once read that when a dog wanted to play, it brought a "toy" to its owner, and when it liked a certain food, it stuck out its tongue showing a satisfied expression.

Therefore, in this case, the dog knows its target public very well. It communicates and receives a response.

Once I was watching the series Seinfeld when the following joke was told:

> ***Dogs are the leaders of the planet. If you see two life forms, one of them is taking a poop, the other one's carrying it for him, who would you assume is in charge?***

One day, my wife told me she saw a woman chewing out her dog. She squatted down, pointed her finger right in front of the dog's face and saw authoritatively:

Look into my eyes when I'm talking to you!

The impression my wife had was that the dog was having fun with this situation.

Curiously, in Brazil during the 1990s, then Minister of Labor Antonio Magri was heavily criticized by the press for declaring that *"Dogs are also human beings"* as a response after being caught taking his dog to the veterinarian inside an official car.

Man's best friend has been promoted to "child," wears people's clothing, receives a "people name," goes to the beauty salon, takes baths in the bathtub, etc. Plainly put: it is the humanization of pets.

If we are capable of humanizing dogs, we are capable of creating a model of God that can meet our needs. We are always "branding" God. We transform him into a product of our own will.

In fact, our will is capable of generating not only religion, but several different gods. To ensure good health, you need money. To go to a good restaurant, you need money. To travel to a tropical paradise, you need money. To win over a beautiful woman, you need money. To buy a fancy sports car, you need money. Fame, health, wealth—they are all the consequence of money.

With a god like this, you need not worry about choosing cheap wines, or the less expensive dish at a restaurant. You need not worry about being rejected by an exuberant woman.

You need not worry about earning recognition because you can buy everything.

If all of this is a blessing, you need to worship the Automatic Teller God—a 24-hour bank with an unlimited balance.

When he was five years old, my son did not understand why whenever he asked us to buy him a more expensive toy, we always had an excuse, and we finally ended up telling him that we could not buy it because we did not have the money.

One day, he said he knew how to make money: he just needed to go to automatic teller machine with his grandmother and slide the debit card through. He really believed that in order to get money, you just needed to have a card and go to the ATM.

But he knew that deep down he had a theophany. He saw a god, or actually the statue of a god, that governs the world. The adoration he witnessed worked as follows: you insert the card into the belly of this god, enter the correct password (the magic word) and he then vomits from his mouth a package of US $100 bills for all eternity.

This god is the god idealized by the world. The god Money. Everything you do in life to obtain favors from this god means worshiping Mammon.

Who is Mammon? It is a word from the Canaanite people that refers to a divinity of greed and money. It was worshiped by the Canaanites, but has transcended the centuries, since it is worshiped still today at several different financial centers worldwide. Where there exists a demand for money, there is a Canaanite altar.

Yeshua talks about two types of spirits—the spirit of God's will and the spirit of Mammon's will.

He says in Matthew 6:24 that it is not possible to serve two Lords. In other words, your heart will lean toward one or the other, because it is not possible to balance the two. If you focus on money, you focus on Mammon and will ask this god for more money without knowing what you are, in fact, asking him for.

This is entirely conflicting with God's will over your life. Yeshua needs to be your Lord and money a mere tool.

God knows man; he knows his target public so well that he sent his own word to live among us. He always knew that we would create guidelines and rules that would drive us away from the word.

In Isaiah 29:13, God himself leaves this clear.

> ***And the Lord said, because this people come near to me with their mouths, and give honor to me with their lips, but their heart is far from me, and their fear of me is false, a rule given them by the teaching of men.***

Mammon is the result of a branding of values that lie in opposition to biblical values. The worshiping of this god is not easily perceived. In fact, it is quite hard for someone to identify this altar in his or her life.

The voice that tempted Yeshua in the desert, demanding miracles, and suggesting shortcuts is a voice that incites us towards violence and also whispers in our ears. This is the difference between the way people live naturally (full of concern and anxiety, the "self-help" man), and the way that God planned for us to live: free of all that excess baggage. And once again excess baggage costs money. It is uncomfortable and gets in the way.

Faith in God gives us the advantage to view our lives from the certainty of God's perspective. The faith that pleases God is the faith of certainty. You cannot live constantly with stress.

How much time have we lost ruminating about situations of the past, thinking about what or what not to do, if something will work out or not, if we will be successful or not, if they will accept us or not. And in function of this, our heads simmer more than a boiling kettle, full of every type of useless thought possible that take us nowhere, but rather destroys the mind and makes it slow, dispersed, and confused, without any discernment or power of reaction.

No more stress, no more insecurity. It is now time to re-examine our values. It is time to recycle.

CHAPTER 6

Unlocking the Cave

A highly qualified but unemployed woman applies for a job and is in the middle of the selection process. During the interview an experienced Human Resources analyst questions her. With a great deal of cordiality and astuteness, learned through years of experience at the head of the HR sector, the interviewer analyzes the woman, leafing through her résumé while he asks her questions.

Finally, he asks why she was fired from her last job. With a climate of tension in the air, the woman suddenly changes, her eyes becoming moist, her face turning red in an undecipherable mixture of anger and sadness, and begins to unleash her rotating machine gun, alleging that she was victim of a complex, orchestrated conspiracy created by evil and merciless minds that heartlessly planned for her dismissal. And of course she speaks very badly of her former company. The interviewer feigns great interest and attention, but the truth is that he is not the least bit interested. He draws stars, circles, triangles and squares and scribbles on the paper. He is not even moved by her crying. To the contrary, his logic is simple. If she speaks poorly of the former company, she is likely to speak poorly of his company as well.

Her truth is not the truth of the story, but simply a version of it. The interviewer does not have time to check, since there are countless résumés on top of his desk, and he will choose the easiest solution.

She should have said: "*I liked working there. I learned a lot, but I am ready for new challenges.*"

The interviewer may even think highly of a sincere person, but he prefers to hire positive ones.

To be positive, you must not be afraid of life. You cannot blame the world. It is easier to free yourself from all responsibility. The idea that the problem lies within us frightens us terribly. This makes us extremely scared, but we must face it head on.

Feeling fear in acceptable doses, however, is completely normal and 100% human. However, it is dangerous to be dominated by fear. We live in a generation dominated by fear. Fear of unemployment, being mugged, betrayed, tricked, bankruptcy, poverty, the doctor, ect., or in other words, millions of people dominated by fear, fear of life, of today and of tomorrow and experiencing the consequences of yesterday's fear.

We have this awful fear of making the wrong choices, and the truth is that we are more insecure when it comes to our steps than those of others. We love to decide for others. I see this with my own son. What father doesn't like to make choices for his own son?

When Bruno was little, my wife and I would choose everything for him. We chose the nanny, daycare, school, food, the soccer team he would cheer for, the friends with whom he would play, the clothing, etc. If it were up to me, I could keep on choosing forever, everything from college to the woman he will marry, the house he will live in, and the car he will drive.

Whether my choices are wrong or right, that's irrelevant. When I choose for him, I don't allow him to overcome his own fear. Instead of helping him, I would exercise a significantly negative influence because I would stall his growth process.

During the journey of life, one of the first levels of struggle that you need to overcome is revealing your intimidation to your enemy. Fear is easy to read. If you demonstrate fear, even to an inoffensive poodle, cute and fluffy like cotton, the animal may growl and bark at you as if it were a pit-bull. If a simple dog can perceive this, imagine the major adversaries in our lives.

Unfortunately, or fortunately, the fears that the majority of us have are not real, but primarily imaginary. We live, suffer, get sick, and melt like ice cream on a sunny day, always facing imaginary fears.

According to some dictionaries, fear is an imaginary feeling, one of threat, fright, dread and apprehension. From a spiritual point of view, fear is the absence of love.

Yes, love—so spoken of, sung of, so recited, so cited in prose and verse in so many languages and cultures—it is still an enigma, since it remains so little understood. Love is one of the most overused and demoralized words in all the world's languages. So much confusion arises from the fact that we have only one word to designate love. But can love truly be captured with a simple definition?

Ambrose Bierce, a 19th century US journalist and writer, described love as temporary insanity, cured by matrimony or by removing the patient from the influences that affect him or her in such way. Obviously this ailment is not love, but rather passion—something quite different.

Love is inevitably confused as a sentiment that transcends logic, that transcends reason, that transcends our domain, but which is actually driven by reason itself. Love serves as a motivating agent that leads us toward affection, interest, and consequently, fondness.

Antoine Saint Exupéry, a French aviator and famous author of the book *The Little Prince*, said:

> ***Love is the only thing that grows as it is shared.***

What is interesting about this phrase is that he speaks of a mathematics that goes in the opposite direction to logic. Division normally reduces the size of "pieces," but here it has a multiplying effect. Another equally interesting characteristic is that, according to the apostle Paul, who is actually Rabbi Shaul (one of the least understood people in history); love is neither invasive nor boring. It is not sticky, it is not impatient, it is not uncontrolled; it is not scandalous and much less possessive. Who has never heard or read the following phrase:

> ***Love your neighbor as you love yourself.***

So what love is this? Love that is an order? Or is it an option? Observe how a phrase with so few words can be so deep, a perfect transmission of a crucial teaching from God that is within our reach. This love means loving others unconditionally to only later try and understand them. This focus reminds us of the figure of a mother swaddling her newborn son, beginning a coexistence marked by full acceptance and trust.

Love is a decision, an aggregating force of respect, solidarity, and the perception of the virtue inherent to every human being, to the detriment of the negative aspects that also constitute the essence of all of us. It is easy to love those who we like, but it is harder to like those for whom we have still not developed affection. Both cases require effort, discipline, and focus since without love we would not be social beings. It is possible to love in quantity and diversity; we can build bridges that allow for convergence between opposites.

It is easy to love our children, parents, spouses, and friends, but feeling the same thing for strangers and people who do not share our values is something complicated, since it is not natural and requires effort and persistence.

Love is a commandment. It is an order and not just a feeling. Our interest and our action should be aligned, but this does not happen. If the logic of love presumes that we must love ourselves first, it is important that we truly love ourselves, since if we are to love our neighbor as much as we love ourselves and we hate ourselves, we will inevitably sow the hate and the repression that lurks within us. If we do not love our own life, then we cannot love other lives. Where there is no love, there is hate. Hate attracts fear, since the two walk hand in hand.

Love is an efficient antidote for fear. By loving life, loving God, your neighbor, and yourself, fear disappears completely.

We react to fear in different ways. When the danger is real, the life preservation feeling, which is an innate and primitive instinct, explodes within us and leads us to fight for survival, awaking a capacity for instinctive reaction.

Fear makes us weak; it debilitates us, turns us into cowards, and makes us draw back. It can even provoke physical reactions, such as the release of adrenaline, an accelerated heartbeat, the shakes, and significant weight changes. This excessive adrenaline—which in situations of danger benefits us, making us more alert, shortening our reaction time and better irrigating our muscles and brain—is also harmful over the long term, knocking us down, since it inevitably leads us to stress.

Fear acts as a drug that harms us. It is the same thing as overdoses of the toxins produced by our minds, with a fatal and destructive effect. We live in a society of people addicted to fear. This drug has not been duly identified and there are no support groups for this dependence that is almost chemical.

Fear makes us feel sorry for ourselves. It brings with it a horrible feeling, as if the paralyzing gas of self-pity had been sprayed all over our faces. The sensation evolves into self-commiseration, which shifts the center of the universe in our direction. In this parallel universe, everything revolves around us and everything must work our way, and not as God wants.

Our ignorance of life makes us imagine that the world is outlined geometrically, as if a giant compass had created the limits of the universe. We place the needle of this compass in our bellybuttons and use it to trace the circumference of the world. This space determines our ego and defines the center of the universe, and it is in this region that our misery and mental weakness reign. It is the region of self-commiseration. A collateral effect of the high doses of fear produced by our "me." This effect destroys us to the point of grinding our bones into infinite micro particles, corroding our structure, and making us look like a gelatinous mass that complains about life and constantly drags along the ground.

It reminds me of a cartoon from my childhood, a pair consisting of a lion always full of marvelous plans and a miserable, boring hyena. They entertained me at home in the mornings, repeating that same infamous phrase:

Oh me … Oh my … Oh dear …

Sometimes, the hyena also said:

This will never work.

It is necessary for us to leave the region where self-commiseration and uncontrolled pessimism reign. This "syndrome of the complaining hyena" has to be ended. Everyone who suffers from this malady feels sorry for themselves and expects compassion from the rest of the world.

Announcing our problems to the four winds is a complete waste of time. Most people who listen to us are not truly concerned with what ails us, and the few who really do listen are happy that we have problems, since they intuitively perform a critical analysis between our situation and their own problems. They are greatly relieved to discover that they are not the only ones confronting adversity.

***

Who has never felt insecure about making a decision, afraid of making a mistake? I am talking here about the fear of important decisions, fear of changing jobs, fear of changing type of activity, fear of getting married, fear of having kids, fear of failing at love, of failing as a father, of failing as a spouse …

Fear of failure makes people indecisive. We have a gigantic fear of making a mistake and being rejected. We are afraid of dealing with error. If we were born with the certainty that there would be no failures in our lives, our achievements would certainly be infinite, since we would not fear carrying the shame of our error.

I invite you to try a mental exercise. Focus all of your concentration on a single thought, making every possible effort to distract yourself form the world and picture a situation.

Think of something very simple, like a piece of fruit, more precisely a lemon—a corpulent, fat, and pleasant-looking lemon. Picture its rounded shapes in your mind; carefully observe its texture and the color of its rind. In this mental construction allow the lemon to remain static at the center of your imaginary visual field.

Now imagine a knife. Not just any knife, but a beautiful and powerful one, one that every great chef dreams about owning, whose blade resembles a sword forged in the hardened steel used by the Samurai and sharpened with utmost care.

Pick up the knife and begin to cut the lemon, slicing it slowly down the middle. Watch how the fruit's juice squirts from the blade, which cuts the lemon so easily, as if it were cutting through butter.

Once the fruit is cut, quickly pick up a succulent part, bursting with the purest lemon juice. Lift it up over your head and squeeze it tightly, pressing the slices until the juice spills uniformly into your mouth. Feel the acidic taste that fills your mouth, drenching your tongue.

If it were possible to take a photo of your face with a digital camera right at the instant that your imagination squeezed the juice into your mouth, you would be able to see your expression of disgust. Note how you are salivating right at this very moment. Surprising, isn't it? If your thoughts during a simple exercise can produce this physical reaction in you, imagine what fear can do to your life.

The truth is that we are the fruit of our thoughts. We are what we think we are. We are what we want to be. Our reality is carefully designed by what we think, since it reflects what we believe: our values and convictions. Some call this the "secret," others "vibrations," some say that everything is "malleable energy," and still others call it the "law of attraction," but the fact is that you create your own reality through faith.

Strangely, we tend to use our capacity to create a reality with perceptions and thoughts that harm us. Rare are those blessed with spiritual intelligence, capable of constructing a positive reality that benefits them and gives them hope. We are extremely self-destructive when the topics that permeate our thoughts are related to our interests. We lack discipline and perseverance.

There is a major war within a world that we do not know very well. It is not a parallel universe. It is our sub-conscious. And this war is not small; it is greater than all the wars waged in the history of the world, where soldiers carry arms; it is bigger than the war on drugs, than the war against corruption, the war against hunger, and the war against global warming.

Within this scenario that develops in our minds, we are the costume designers, stage managers, directors and characters. When we experience this excessive worrying, anguish, endless and repetitive doubts, depression, anger, or guilt, we sabotage our own lives, hindering our capacity to react. We create a dead end, where our thoughts are like enriched uranium at a nuclear plant working at maximum capacity. It is pure energy, circulating through a complex and intricate nervous system. A military division at war could represent each problem, and that is why there are battalions fighting in our heads. We have to end this type of thinking so that we may have peace and freedom. We must have full mastery over our minds. If we pick up shovels and excavation equipment, and act like careful archeologists researching the origins of thought, we would need to go to its Western cradle, which is Greece. Socrates, Plato, and the Sophists represent the foundations of Greek thinking. The apogee of classic Greece occurred 500 years before Yeshua.

For the Sophists, knowledge began with the senses. According to this form of reasoning, knowledge is accessible to all, since everyone has the capacity to think. One of the topics of heated debate was investigating whether knowledge was obtained through the senses. In public squares, in the Agoras, Greek democracy was expressed through oratory and eloquence. The more the discussion and the more the speech, the more the capacity for reasoning was exercised. Not everyone thought that way, however. What is interesting is that Socrates, the greatest of all Greek thinkers, left nothing written. What is known about him is what Plato reported. Socrates was sentenced to death because he preached against Greek democracy, and in the ancient texts he played the role of the character expressing Plato's will.

For the members of the academy, sentiments were misleading since they deformed reality, while the only reference for knowledge came from reason.

Let us look now at one of the most interesting stories from the Greek heyday, in the purest style of Agoras of Athens, which I have taken the liberty of changing and adapting, recreating a simpler allegory of the cave, whose essence is not lost:

Imagine a hypothetical mini-world where there is a group of four men who live confined and chained to the back of a moist, poorly lit cave. In this world, they have never been in contact with the outdoors. This dark cave is home to small rodents and bats and a small stream of drinkable water flows along the feet of this group of people. They have practically always lived there and do not have any recollections or memories of the outside world.

In a tedious and hardly creative routine, they are content to watch the distorted shadows on a wall at the back of the cave, which gives them a sort of ghostly aspect, as if it were a trashy movie playing in a theater without any type of comfort. The sound is terrible, since the soundtrack of their daily lives is distorted. Through the narrow hole of access to the cavern, it is possible to hear disjointed noises that blend with the sounds of flowing water and animals. The echo and the shadows are the backdrop of a mythical world, an outside world, something that exists only in their imagination.

One day, one of the four became outraged with his life. He began to break through the chains that bound him, and because they were rusted, they finally broke. His body was free, but more importantly than this, his mind was also free. He then turned to his companions in captivity: *Let's go, let's get out of here, nothing chains us here anymore!*

His companions answered: *Are you crazy? Why would we take the risk of leaving here? Here we have everything.*

We lack nothing ... the world is that which we have, what we hear, what we see, what we smell, what we touch and what we taste. You cannot leave here, because this is what we have guaranteed, it is real, and you cannot take the risk of leaving in search of something that does not exist. Your ideas bother us; they bring disorder and subvert our peace of spirit. Let us live as we want to live.

The man who had removed his chains decided to leave anyway. There was no time to lose. He followed the tenuous, thin stream of light for hours until he reached the entrance to the cave and suddenly, a shock! He was hardly able to bear the clarity that bothered his eyes, as he was so used to the darkness. After some time he began to see a new reality, where there was grass, abundant vegetation, where he could hear the beautiful sounds of birds singing, with pleasant weather, different animals, people walking and talking. The guttural and distorted sounds he had heard in the cavern were now understandable and melodic. The new world initially bothered him, but he persevered. He wanted to try; he wanted to feel. He ate fruits and watched children playing from afar. He looked up at the blue sky, which amazed him with its diversity of colors, since the world of the cavern was monochromatic and grey.

Despite his boldness, after coming into contact with the new reality, he tried to deny it and it took him a while to accept it. After overcoming his fear, however, he returned to the cave and told the others in detail everything he had seen, trying in vain to convince his companions to adventure out on this journey. They did not accept his offer. They found it hard to imagine this change; they resisted thinking about the possibility of transformations and called him crazy. Conflict became inevitable and they ended up killing the one who tried to change them.

Through this story we can see that we are chained to a reality created by our own feelings and we are not willing to produce another reality based on ideas and thinking. We are the Sophists of the 21st century, even though Plato showed us that it is ideas that produce reality. When we dare and adventure to produce it, when we truly want to assume control of our lives, our lack of discipline ends up hindering us from doing it, since we become our own saboteurs, creating something that does us no good. We are our own executioners. We put the chains around ourselves.

This point is so crucial that even before the most important creators of Greek thought presented their ideas, there was already someone in the Middle East known for his wisdom. King Solomon forces us to pay attention to he who was wisest of all. The bible underpins Solomon's thinking, since it declares that there never had existed nor would there ever exist someone like him. Solomon knew that nothing is more powerful in the world than the human mind. Your mind matters and how you choose to think will have a major influence on nearly everything that happens in your life. The Bible says: ***"As he [a man] thinks in his heart, so is he"*** (Proverbs 23:7). So we are the fruit of your own thoughts. You are what your mind imagines you to be.

The idea is that fact produces reality. Something exists only when we understand and idealize it. Appearance camouflages essence. The senses only perceive appearance, and never essence. This is very important, since essence is thought.

We must be the auditors of our thoughts. Discipline and control are required for these thoughts to be positive. Good thoughts generate good results, and if they are favorable, the fruits are good. Good harvests indicate a life of success.

We came to the world to bear fruits. If we have only bad thoughts, the fruit of our life will have the flavor of defeat. If we have good thoughts, the flavor of the fruit will be sweet, succulent, and good.

What reality do we produce? Good or bad? The power that we possess is enormous, but we have the bad habit of ruining everything, since we mask fear and uncertainty in our ideologies. Some may even say that our thoughts transcend our control. I say that we do have control mechanisms. If we are strong enough to go on diets to control our appetite, then theoretically we are strong enough to patrol our brain activity. If we look for the strength that comes from God, we can have a harmonious life. Our thoughts must be totally concentrated on recovering objectives; we must carry on forward and not give up.

If we seek success, the focus of our thoughts should be centered on God, so that based on this guarantee, we may realize and materialize our will. This alignment between our effort and God's will is crucial for ensuring that our objectives and effort will not be in vain.

Imagine that you have met someone interesting, and that you think that she may be the great love of your life, a person suitable and down-to-earth enough for you to spend the rest of your days with. However, this person does not return your feelings. She does not have the same perception as you do. There is no reciprocity. What is the use of imagining, praying, concentrating and so ardently desiring to win this person's heart? It is not enough for you to create your reality, since even if you really believe in it, it will be impossible to achieve your objective without the agreement and consent from God.

It is hard to believe that an intelligent person like yourself, who has received the knowledge from God, who knows that everything is possible for those who believe and who knows that it is possible to move mountains, wastes his time and energy concentrating on something that is less than you deserve.

That's right! You deserve someone who wants to be at your side. Why lower yourself, getting hooked on someone who does not know that you exist and who lives focused on another person? A macro analysis of this situation, observing all the actors and impacts on those involved, leads us to conclude that the decision orchestrated from a relationship with God occurs on the basis of a careful analysis of the objectives and needs of all participants. It is a very complex resolution, but one which directly influences your life and that of other people. Therefore, if the indifference of the one you love continues, it is a clear sign that there was no approval from God and, accordingly, feeding this type of desire unleashes emotional attrition.

Why concentrate on wanting a Ferrari Testarossa? Janis Joplin, a white singer with a black woman's voice who marked the history of blues forever, composed a song that became a major success, where she claimed that she wanted a Mercedes with the following characteristics:

> ***Lord, won't you buy me a Mercedes Benz? My friends all drive Porsches, I must make amends. Worked hard all my lifetime, no help from my friends, so Lord, won't you buy me a Mercedes Benz.***

God, however, did not buy her a Mercedes Benz.

She, who envied the Porsches of her friends, said that something needed to be done. If God holds all power and can do anything, why didn't he give Joplin that which she wanted? Why does he not give man what he desires? Why not give mortal man what he wants with refined sophistication?

Even better, why does God not recreate the universe? Why is there not a voice echoing from heaven, saying:

> ***Mortal man, remove the sandals from your feet and listen carefully: I will recreate a new Universe in six days! I will place you there as the new Adam, and to ensure that you will not be alone; I will place by your side a very nice, pretty girl named Eve. You guys will have all the best, a 3D-TV with cable and a garage in Eden with a Ferrari Testarossa with the insurance paid. However, the Ferrari was expensive, and after going over the budget, there was no money left to put a fence around the tree of knowledge of good and evil. This is why I command you: Under no circumstance let the woman eat the apple again like the last one did. Pay attention, new Adam, be smart and careful, and do not let her run up the credit card with designer label clothes.***

Do you still want this Ferrari? Or would you prefer a Porsche? You have not received it yet? Why not? Because you deserve something bigger than a designer label and status symbol, which will basically serve to create appearances and to be shown off as a trophy to your friends. It is not something that you want for its usefulness, but rather to give meaning to your life. After all, the opinion of others is still very important, even if you refuse to admit it. You deserve better recognition and the respect of others, but not for the car that you own. You deserve something grandiose that is achieved with your own efforts, which is why only through God you will obtain the power to discern the true, deep down needs of the human soul.

The act of praying is fundamentally associated with the need to focus our decisions based on God's will. That is why we pray: to align our will with his permission. What is interesting is that there is a great spiritual secret guaranteeing us that when there is resonance between man and God, our desire is realized. God is not a genie in a lamp found by Aladdin, who grants three wishes without any criteria. You can ask a genie in a lamp for a winning lottery ticket, a private jet, a paradisiacal island in the Caribbean, but let us agree that it will be very hard for you to trip in the desert and find this lamp. It is better and much safer for you to follow the flowchart from God and seek this resonance that transforms:

> ***This is the trust that we have in him, who, if we ask for something, according to his will, he hears us. And if we know that he hears us in everything we ask for, we know that we have achieved what we have requested of him.***

In this case doubt is a benefit. If we are too sure our steps are already decided, but if we seek the resonance with God, our doubt dissipates and reality is transformed.

When a baby is learning to walk, it falls down frequently until it builds up enough confidence. Babies, however, are better and more courageous than we are, since they fall, cry, and get up again. We sometimes get stuck on the crying part. Tears bring dismay. When we make a mistake, we have the tendency to believe that we are failures. Everyone makes mistakes, but this does not mean that they are failures. We must accept that we have weak points and strong points. We should not open our arms to condemnation. When we feel weak, let us allow God to be our strength.

Dismay is a mental pattern that we cannot accept for our lives, and that is why we must seek strength and courage in God to balance our diet of thoughts.

Dismay destroys hope; it gets in the way of our journey. We are prone to stop and give up in the middle of the voyage. How many people were happy, spontaneous, loved to live, were excited to go out and see friends, but then became unhappy people who no longer leave their homes and feel inferior to everyone else? People who currently only want to be alone, sleep, and cry. For these people, life no longer has any charm, since they have lost their courage and are too lazy to believe in the perspectives for victory that emanate from God.

Losing our courage means becoming weak. That is why we must remain firm.

Is it possible to imagine Yeshua himself in the middle of fasting saying: *It was hard!* Or going even further and stating: *The pain of humanity will be unbearable?* Have you ever imagined how frustrating it would be to go on preaching and wandering, without a home, without a roof, without a bed to sleep in at night, with your friends and allies weakened and betraying you? Imagining his dismay is imagining something inconceivable.

Thoughts of victory cannot coexist with thoughts focused on difficulties and obstacles. Success follows suffering. And success comes after work. The only place where success comes before work is in the dictionary.

Correct thoughts arm us for battle. Going to battle with the wrong thoughts is asking to be gunned down; it means accepting defeat before the battle even begins. Thinking is based on belief, on believing. However, if we observe carefully the belief that manifests itself in many people today is synonymous with the repetition of clichés that we learn and which proliferate in our daily lives—clichés that are recited as if they were real mantras. It is canned belief, a byproduct of laziness. This belief comes with a label that leads the consumer to repeat phrases in such a way that they "manipulate" the heavens and earth.

It is like a bag of potato chips, the kind you can find in supermarkets and convenience stores. You buy a bag to eat in front of the television. You do not really know why you are eating the chips, and deep down you feel deep remorse because you could be eating something more healthy and nutritious. Even so, you eat until the very last chip is gone, because they taste so good. This "canned" belief uses slogans that supposedly move God's arm depending on the tastes of the one in charge. The result? You are bound to fail.

Correct thinking is a process of brainstorming leading to a conclusion that brings absolute conviction. A conclusion that pulses ardently and which expresses our real inner being.

The people of Israel lamented and complained for 40 years, fearful of new challenges and groaning about every difficulty they experienced. A generation needed to be renewed since it was tied to a vision marked by difficulties and obstacles. There are thoughts of defeat that are extremely harmful to our lives. They are patterns of brain activity that multiply impossibilities, such as when we silently affirm to ourselves:

> ***I won't be able to. It is really hard. I always fail. I will not make it. I am stupid. Nothing changes. I am tired of trying; I will never reach it.***

Keywords like "never" and "always" are absolute. Statements such as: "I will never pass the test" or "I am always a failure," are extremely destructive and cruel. If we practice this type of thinking, then we are sentencing and condemning ourselves, and we will certainly be defeated, eternally giving up and depressed.

If we change our way of thinking, we will be freed. After all, weakness is not a stigma, it is not a crime, and much less is it a pathological evil or incurable disease. It is merely a word that expresses the sentiment of the result. Favorable results indicate success, and unfavorable results indicate weakness. What is the weight of this? Who establishes the weight of this expression? Words do not have meanings in and of themselves, but they express the values we attribute to them. They are human conventions, circumscribed by the mechanics of language. And if language expresses our thoughts, then we should be very careful and attentive. Thinking, picturing, and especially feeling causes our vibratory state to change and makes us construct a new reality.

Change your vocabulary to change your life.

Modifying our speech is crucial for transformation. It is the first step. If a boy says: "I will be at the head of the team if I train a lot and dedicate myself," instead of "I will never be at the head of the team," then he will be putting into practice one of the most useful teachings from God.

Pay attention to this important point: *Thinking hurts!*

Constructing consistent thoughts means making an effort. This is why television is so popular. It requires feelings, but not mental effort. TV has a sedative effect, since it numbs our capacity to organize our thoughts, interacting in the interior of our passivity. We can only understand our essence through reasoning.

It is like our lives are a reflection of a real "Matrix" film—a parallel dimension. We imagine a world of pain, darkness, and defeats. We are afraid. We are gargling lemonade though it does not exist. Once we have identified reality, however, it is impossible to live inside the "Matrix."

We have the obsessive idea of creating alternative worlds and we never clearly discern what is real and what is illusory.

So, how should we deal with our fears? The solution is simple. We need only believe in God's promises. But remember that believing is dependent on a principle of obedience.

The word "promise" is one that is difficult for us to accept, since it loses its strength as we suffer from the treachery of people who did not honor their promises to us. This case, however, is quite different, because God promises because he wants to, not because he needs to.

Isaiah, a prophet and one of the most interesting figures in human history, transmitted the teachings that he received from the Creator:

Do not fear, for I am with you; do not be dismayed, because I am your God. I will strengthen you and help you; I will uphold you with my righteous right hand.

Courage is a major differential between winners and those who give up. Decide the group you want to fit into. Receive this courage. Yes, receive it. It does not come from within you.

Obstacles are those scary things that you see when you cannot keep your eyes focused on your objective. Obstacles are factors that keep dreams from becoming a reality. Obstacles separate utopia and reality.

Wisdom from God makes us realize that objectives and purposes in harmony with God's plans cannot be destroyed by the insecurity created by a world that rejects this instruction. We cannot be distracted by looking to the sides.

Humankind's greatest challenge is not exploring the depths of the ocean, nor is it reaching the frontiers of the solar system. Rather, it is to look in the mirror, face yourself and affirm with all your might: *I know you!*

Man tries to know himself, and this enigma becomes increasingly difficult to decipher. Understanding our essence leads us to identify our fellow man. Our interests are shaped by the understanding of our identity, even because identity is what we think we are, what we want to be and what we allow ourselves to be.

To define ourselves, we need others, since we are a compound created by the environment. We are part of the whole; we influence the whole and we are influenced by it. We do not live alone, we do not educate ourselves alone, we do not learn alone, we do not achieve success alone, and we do nothing important alone.

Sigmund Shlomo Freud said:

> ***Give me the first seven years of a child and keep the rest!***

However, it is during adolescence that our identity blossoms and our differences in relation to the "other" become more evident. As we mature, we more clearly define our ideas and values.

That which makes us different does not necessarily complement us. To the contrary, it creates a giant abyss. When we construct our identity, it is natural for us to pull away from those whose values are different. Creating enemies is part of the self-awareness process.

We also need to have allies; we need to believe that our family is better, that our friends our better, that our group is better than that of the others. When united we are strong; we have cohesion. Recognition and approval of the group to which we belong directly affects our self-esteem.

When we are young, it is normal to have frequent battles in our head, like jealousy, envy, and competition. This is a characteristic of insecurity. If we are 100% secure in relation to our own value and importance, the success of others does not make us jealous.

We accept reality, even if we do not like it. Envy is a natural feeling. It makes no one noble, it is nothing to be proud of, but it is part of every breath we take, our feeding, our way of life, whether or not we like this fact. And of course, despite being a reality, we cannot be guided nor driven by envy.

All of us, in our weaknesses, have at one time or another felt envious of others. In most cases, however, we are capable of seeing that we are wrong and we can correct these deviations, repressing this type of feeling. If we are still unable, then we can adopt a Plan B, repudiating it and seeking help in the power that emanates from God. Feeling the need to compare ourselves with others will certainly make our lives more difficult unnecessarily. It is a waste of time and energy. This envy can bring terrible results, since it robs us of our motivation and focus.

Insecurity, however, is not a characteristic associated exclusively with youth. Often we are older and with a little less. This envy grows to the point that we are left hung up, frustrated and upset.

During our lives we will always encounter two types of people. Those who wait for things to happen and those who make things happen. In other words there are people who control fear and people who are controlled by it.

Those who are controlled by fear normally wait, they are accommodated, satisfied with everything around them. They do not try to do something different, purely and simply because they are afraid to fail, and because of this, they miss out on important experiences, locking themselves away in the comfort of their own homes and still giving thanks to God that they are protected from the world. Those that control and master their fear are those who make things happen. They are considered crazy and inconsistent; they are misunderstood and ridiculed. They do not consider failure to be a dead-end, but rather the beginning of a new journey. They face their defeats, failures and errors as part of reality and life itself. They let themselves dream, dare, and do.

Regardless of how mature we may be, we always fail in one area or another, and failure brings with it guilt, remorse, accusation, and the dangerous state of self-pity.

The lessons that were taught to us, the education we received, the expectations others have of us, all of this is the focus of our success. Failure, on the other hand, is rarely addressed.

Accordingly, we mature unprepared, without knowing how to react to it.

Sooner or later, however, we end up discovering and experiencing it, since even the greatest entrepreneurs fail countless times before achieving success.

Dismay is a mental pattern that we cannot accept for our lives. If we learn that we have a unique and personal plan for our lives, we do not need to compare ourselves to anyone else. We will not be insecure. We will not be controlled by fear, and we will avoid failure.

CHAPTER 7

DEBRANDING THE MYTH

After God created order in Eden, the perfect scenario for his work, he finally created man to inhabit the center of his will.

The foundations of a new order were laid.

What is order? It is a structure not generated by chance, with a specific objective and with rules and reactions. Human beings want order, not disorder. They want something that can generate predictability. The world wants actions and reactions.

Nobody wants to live in disorder, where law and property are not respected and where life is threatened at any given moment. Order preserves promises; it preserves life; it preserves ownership. If it were not this way, what would be the reasons for studying, working, marrying, having children and living?

Order is an arrangement of human life to guarantee "basic objectives", such as:

1) Preserving life
2) Fulfilling the truth—which in Latin is a concept known as "*pacta sunt servanda*" (pacts being fulfilled)
3) Guaranteeing property

What order would exist if I walked down the street and a scoundrel decided to stab me because he didn't like the way I looked? No order, therefore this would breach my first principle, since my life was threatened.

What order would exist if I made payments to a consortium and after 48 payments they told me that I had not contracted anything? If I pay for bread at the bakery and then the guy at the counter tells me that I had not paid? No order, since this would breach my second principle, since the pacts (agreements) were not fulfilled. What order would there be if I arrived home and a group of homeless people was in the living room watching TV, drinking from my glasses and saying that the house was no longer mine? No order, as this would breach the third principle, since my property was not being respected.

Man was created to supervise this order. To create order he has the authority to dominate creation. God grants this authority. God created the world in five days and on the sixth day he created man, gave him authority and declared that everything was very good. Good in the sense of excellence and perfection. Finally, on the seventh day he rested. We are taught to rest on this day in order to contemplate and reflect on the universe of the Creator.

Order is even concerned about our rest. God created an orderly world to establish man in a paradise of utopist perfection and finally to rest with him. The *Shabbat*, which is the seventh day, is a symbol of plenitude, limitless perfection, communion, and harmony between creatures and the Creator. However, man leaves Eden and this is when disorder begins to reign.

Many years later, several generations after Eden, in a world increasingly dominated by the search for self-interest and exacerbated individuality, a man named Goliath emerged among the Philistines who spread fear and terror.

If personal marketing can be seen as a process of conception, planning and execution of actions that lift a person to a distinguished place, then Goliath was the pioneer of personal marketing. He knew how to stir up a crowd and his enemies like no one else. He knew how to get attention, how to plan his self-promotion in details and how to transform this into power, creating fear and terror in his adversaries.

He created an image that made everyone around him feel completely inferior. Without any help from a press office or advertising agency, without the use of any type of media, Goliath turned himself into a myth. Goliath did not feel uncomfortable about speaking in public, since he was a great communicator. The best communication meets its objectives, and Goliath obtained success because he knew how to communicate, how to influence, and how to threaten and disseminate terror among the Israelites. His words had an effect. They were lethal; they catalyzed and propagated fear. It was the propaganda of the foreign, failure, impossible, unattainable, and the insurmountable obstacle.

Goliath threatened and challenged the people of Israel for 40 days, in the morning and in the afternoon—a daily ritual that paired off the armies and defiled the Israelites exactly at their time of prayer. When these words are associated with an image and adequate techniques and methods, they are enormously efficient, since they paralyze the listener, neutralizing his or her power to react.

The people of Israel were paralyzed, anchored, and stranded like a transatlantic ocean liner that, as it gets dangerously close to the beach, gets stuck on a sandbar. The psychological massacre suffered by the Israelites led them down into a deep anguish, a form of daily torture, a fright never before felt.

However, the solution from God, as always, came from the least expected source. The then young David, youngest of seven children of Jesse, was making a delivery, at the order of his father, which was to take food to his brothers who were in the battlefield. He was responsible for the chain of supply, the logistics on the battlefield. By chance, he found himself in a scenario in which a giant named Goliath challenged and spread fear throughout the entire army of Israel. At that moment, David, armored with extraordinary boldness and optimism, assumed the commitment of battling against that giant in a heroic fashion. And it was at this moment that David revealed a faith that did not falter when faced with an enemy or a challenge. It displayed optimism for its people, who had only seen defeat before them.

Goliath's personal marketing did not look upon David's image favorably. Goliath's projected image did not tune into David's receptor. He changed the station.

Most of us are defeated on the eve of the battle, so when we come face-to-face with some problem, with some giant of life, we accept defeat and give up even before the battle begins. Our minds are producers of giants; we increase the size of our obstacles to something far bigger than they actually are. This negativist vision of reality contributes to making us vulnerable when it comes to being knocked out by the adversary. There were those, however, who did not cave into negativism.

David was a young man who was not afraid of challenges. He convinced King Saul that he could face Goliath, and so Saul offered him weapons and armor. But David did not use these resources to fight Goliath. He rejected the armor. It was heavy and uncomfortable. That is why David headed out for battle without it, taking with him only a slingshot and a few stones that he had plucked out of a stream.

However, David had vision and knew that we always fail when we wear only human armor. The armor containing the weapons of pride, arrogance, and self-sufficiency will lead us to defeat, since it is vulnerable and incapable of defending us.

David was not the type of person who waited for the giant to attack him; he attacked first. Unfortunately, we do not use David's tactics in our lives. Rather, we wait to be struck first and only react afterwards. Our problem is that we are the people on the defensive end, in other words, we only begin to fight after the problem, and situation or circumstance has already become a giant. And then, it is usually too late.

We have to face the problem while it is still small, in order to ensure that it never grows excessively. David knew that the best defense strategy was attack, and by studying steps and strategies, we learn that by acting preventively, the chances of being successful increase exponentially.

Who is this uncircumcised Philistine to confront the armies of the Living God?

David had a pact, an alliance with God, whose external symbol was circumcision, an identification that reflected an effective alliance that lived and pulsed within him.

David's obvious conclusion was that this pact did not exist with Goliath. Therefore, despite his handicap, David was able to go into battle without fear.

Now, the personal marketing changes sides. Now it is David who chooses his words well and screams authentically, without fear and without doubt.

> ***You come with your sword, spear and shield. However, I come forward against you in the name of the Lord of Hosts, God of the army of Israel that you have challenged, because this battle is God's and he will deliver you into my hands***

Words have power, and even if Goliath did not admit it, he was already impressed with David's audacity and boldness. What card did this guy carry up his sleeve that drove him to exchange effronteries with the giant? At this point, it was obvious that tension and curiosity dominated the air.

When Goliath saw that boy in front of him, he could not help but tease him, but David did not waver. He placed a stone in his slingshot and launched it against the giant. The rock hit Goliath's forehead and he fell to the ground completely defeated. After this David took the giant's sword and used it to cut his head off. When they saw that their hero had been defeated, the army of Philistines, now in panic, fled in complete disorientation and was chased by Saul's men who destroyed them.

David trusted God completely and accordingly had his faith strengthened, since faith is a gift that must be exercised.

There will always be a Goliath in our lives. Just like David, our alternative is to battle—we have no way out. The battle will bring us victory so that this alliance is known to all, since the best marketing is that which reflects the truth and is authentic. Marketing cannot serve to subvert the individual, to recruit personal benefits or to change reality.

It may seem crazy, but sometimes losing is a good thing. Many people get used to victory, and because they feel bad after a defeat, they react and overcome it. Losing is an indication that we are not prepared for certain adversaries and we must train and try even harder.

Over the short term, defeat is bad, but over the long term losing is more profitable for many than winning. Winning only serves to boost the ego momentarily. Alignment with God's will is not a momentary, occasional victory resulting from a vanity that is hungry for successes, which brings fame interweaved with moments of defeat. A solid victory is the legitimate consequence of recognition that the world will have with those who position themselves in alignment with God.

Approximately two thousand years ago Yeshua was born in the village of Bethlehem during the *Sukkoth* festival (Tabernacle). He was the savior so longed for by the world, though even nowadays few people recognize his coming or fully understand its meaning. Even when Yeshua grew up, became mature, and began to unveil the truth, many people found it enormously difficult to believe that it was he to whom the scriptures referred, the long awaited *mashiach*. For these people, Yeshua's profile simply did not fit into the description given by the prophets. The bare naked truth is that many did not believe, nor do they believe today, that he who was "the sent one."

Isaiah spoke about the birth of the messiah 700 years before the event. The people of Israel were looking for a leader that fitted within the molds of neighboring governments, with a strong monarch, a controller of the tensions and social struggles, a king who would defend the kingdom, expand its borders, who would end oppression and neutralize enemies, bringing peace—by force, if necessary. They needed a powerful leader like King David.

All of us are thirsty for kings. Deep down, we are melancholic monarchists. When there are no kings to appoint or queens to adore, our uncontrollable instinct toward veneration leads us to create them easily. We create the "King of Soccer," "King of Fighters," "Queen of the Catwalk," etc. It is amazing how many kings are available in all different sizes, colors, and flavors. And this is how we continue our king manufacturing process.

Not all kings are created for human convenience. Not all kings are the product of a communication and marketing team, which transforms a king into a well packaged product, meeting consumers' needs. King David did not have advisors, lobbyists, a political party structure or treasurers; he was approved and legitimated by God.

David brought peace through victories in major battles. From the giant Goliath to the battles between armies, he was able to align opposite sentiments and characteristics. He had the soul of a poet and the spirit of a warrior, two antagonistic and coexisting qualities. A man who had a certain weakness for women, and accordingly killed, betrayed, and battled but who stripped himself completely bare as described in Psalm 51. His sincere repentance turned him into a man after God's own heart.

***

We live in a world in which everyone seeks a model, an objective, a standard, an ideal, a reality. When we are unable to achieve this reality, we try to escape from it to in order to feel pleasure and joy in a world that exists only in our heads. We create our realities, and many times, they are excessively far from the visible and perceivable world. A very raw example would be a fan of a soccer team that never wins in the real world. He does not care about this, however, because in the virtual world, in videogames, he is able to win, and for him this is sufficient and pleasing enough.

This virtual world is increasingly more tangible and present, especially now when cyberspace is as real as physical space. Virtual companies set up operations in a virtual universe, where people with virtual names and virtual appearances, visit virtual stores in sites where even countries of the real world establish embassies in the virtual world.

Accordingly, reality is an increasingly difficult concept to define.

Every model is an attempt to represent reality. Every theory aims to explain something as being real. The shelves of bookstores are full of books on these topics. However, the model is not always a reality. The paradigms represent the standards to be followed, until they are replaced by models that express reality in the best and most efficient way.

The concept of beauty, for example, is not something unalterable. To the contrary, the definition of what is considered beautiful has varied widely over time.

Today, the nearly anorexic thin type is valued as a commercial strategy, since a rectilinear and slim body type stands out from the clothing and catches even more attention, therefore selling more.

Accordingly, this is the current standard of beauty, and those who best represent it are the models. Some, those who are extremely famous, are no longer just mere models, but rather super models. They are the top models. If the model is someone to be imitated and one of these top models is my model, that is, if by chance my great desire and dream in life was to walk the catwalks and appear in photo shoots, then I would be far from reality. If I were to try to imitate this model even until the final consequences, if I were to try my luck on the catwalk, my heels would break, I would not have the grace, the elegance, the presence, and attitude that they do, and I would not be as beautiful in the photo shoots. Besides this, being a man, I would obviously be grotesque, androgynous, and ridiculous.

Accordingly, the model that displays the beauty of the universe of catwalks and fashion is very far from my reality. If these top models populate the covers of sophisticated fashion magazines, then I am a sad and lamentable reality …

One of the main characteristics and properties of cinema is to create the illusion of reality.

Rock stars are beings that live in a paradise of rebellion. They occupy a position of anti-behavior. They are living legends. They are modern myths, different from those of classic mythology.

The myth is born from the desire to dominate the world, to chase away fear and insecurity, gods and demons. With a poster of his idol on the wall, a “metal head” feels stronger, more tribal. With a soccer star as a myth, you feel like a winner when he wins. Major sports athletes are myths.

Despite this fact, the myth is not capable of stopping the human being from being attracted to him. For example, although it is considered unreal, mythology is maintained and sought out by man even in these days.

Do not assume that myths are something created by stupid people and hollow minds. Regardless of our stage of intellectual development, this function of creating fables is part of our daily life. The mass media works with the desires that exist in our nature, such as super heroes, television stars and famous athletes. Even soap operas deal with the mythical values found inside us. Stars transformed into myths, however, are heroes without any real power. They only exist symbolically in the population's imagination.

Advertising is mythical and, accordingly, creates myths of consumption and happiness based on an ideal. Advertising endorses our repressed desire for myths. Many television commercials create harmonious, beautiful families that are worry-free and happy, eating breakfast cereals that bring them health, joy, energy, prosperity, and success throughout the day.

If the opposite were shown on TV, then certainly the product advertised would never leave the shelves. Therefore, they are heroes without real power, trying to show a reality that does not exist.

However, there is a real power. A hero who is not distanced from our reality, a myth that does not distort that which surrounds us, the *mashiach* (messiah in Hebrew).

Yeshua is the model, created in God's image and resemblance like us, but able to really perform this function masterfully.

He did not seek recognition, glory, honor or personal benefits. He was obedient to a well-defined hierarchy. He had the right and duty to head the process of *Tikkun Olam* and did not try to skirt this responsibility at any moment.

Every principle of authority oscillates between making decisions, giving orders, requiring obedience or simply performing the task to which one is assigned. His authority was not obtained through force or politics, what makes it legitimate is the power and favor that comes from God.

The mashiach was sent to be the model. His objective was to allow for spiritual inclusion by using a logic based on the instruction from God.

Obviously, a project of this magnitude requires carefully calculated procedures. The rewards, when obtained, will outweigh the risks taken. What is interesting is that only he as an individual assumes this burden for the whole process to the benefit of all humanity.

The quest for spiritual advancement is not a search for personal well being, but rather a selective process for cooperating toward a greater good, the *Tikkun Olam* (world repair). We will always need outside help for these repairs to take place. For a collective and globalized *Tikkun* that can be widely encompassing, this need is even more pressing. For this to occur, we need a fixer. This need exists because in the past, in Eden, there were problems whose consequences affect us still today.

God used earth as the raw material for creating the first man in his image and resemblance: Adam, the earth being, he who was created from earth, our first reference and representative. His name comes from the Hebrew word *adamah* (ground). He can be compared to a vase that was created from the dust of the earth. However, this vase did not stand divine light, and that is why it shattered into countless pieces. Adam did not understand the need to remain within a quality standard that would meet God's expectations. We are actually broken vases, and these scattered shards also need to be fixed to ensure the return to the original standard. Adam was the archetype of a person disobedient to God. Adam was the first to embrace the principle of rebellion to the instruction from God. That is why we needed a new Adam, a new reference, a clean vase, a *Tikkun Olam.*

At this moment, a new Adam appears on the scene: a carpenter, who is the very essence of the *Tikkun*. Yeshua's message leaves this clear. It is incredible and truly impressive that even today his influence on men is still being discussed. Especially if we take into account that the distance he traveled during a period of three years was minimal, and also considering that he lived during a period in which there was television, cable, Internet, satellites, radios, billboards, press, or any other type of media.

The consistency of his message is undeniable and does not leave any space for weighted refutation. The discussion of his teachings, the historical record of his life and the theological consequences of his apparition are so important that the media frequently refers to it and the publishing market launches countless books, magazines, and theories about his life. A figure who divides the Western calendar into before and after his birth cannot go unnoticed and cannot leave us indifferent. A unique man; a fascinating message!

Acting and speaking are not connected words. There is an abyss between these two verbs. Speaking is quite easy, especially when we use words that express our opinions. The hard part is expressing what we really want to say through gestures and attitudes. Responsibility for the connection between acting and speaking in a way that allows for the reconstruction of an Adam-like species within the original standard is a major necessity. THE REST FACTOR makes it possible to restore our essence that is, above all, chaotic.

A brief everyday example illustrates how life in and of itself is only an agglomerate of disorganized and non-synchronized situations essentially disconnected from an objective that strives for collective benefit.

Some time ago, a work colleague told me about a vivid incident that he had witnessed. The divine comedy of an absolutely chaotic daily life. Everything happened within a 10-minute interval, while he was waiting for me to give him a ride. I was going to drop him off near a client and we were going to take advantage of the situation to chat a bit.

On a busy street in Rio de Janeiro, where there was a reasonable flow of pedestrians and cars passing by, a bakery and butcher's shop sit side by side. A charitable and well-intentioned woman saw a dog that appeared to be abandoned, poorly cared for and underweight on the corner and decided to go into the butcher's shop and purchase approximately two hundred grams of fresh ground beef.

She happily left the butcher's shop and threw the meat on the sidewalk, where the dog was lying down, right next to the bakery. Of course, the dog got up quickly, walked over to the meat and began to eat it. Certain pedestrians and clients of both establishments, observing the scene of the hungry dog eating the meat, began to grumble and yell, saying that it was absurd and indecent, with so many people suffering from hunger in the world, that a mere dog had been given such luxurious meat.

The bakery manager, extremely irritated, complained out loud about the mess that the animal was making in front of his establishment, since this was driving away his clients. He picked up a broom, drove off the dog, which had already eaten most of the meat, and swept the ground, shoving the rest of the meat into the middle of the street. The dog ran after it, not giving up, and went to the middle of the street to eat what was left.

The street was busy, the traffic did not stop and a taxi appeared out of nowhere and ran over the dog. The taxi continued on its way, not stopping to help the animal. From the back of the bakery, another individual emerged, the cashier, who came running out, screaming desperately, bursting into tears and horrified with the scene, explaining that the dog was hers. She stayed in the middle of the street, holding the bloody dog in her arms, in the middle of moving traffic.

A new commotion: the customers of the butcher's shop and bakery, the pedestrians, and the taxi drivers at the taxi station all started yelling at the women telling her to get out of there quickly and stop acting crazy, because she was in the middle of the street and would be run over. The bakery cashier screamed that the cars can run her over, since her life no longer has any purpose. This incident makes us think. Who was wrong? The woman who bought the meat for the dog, but seemed to ignore the world's hunger? The public, which criticized the charitable woman for ignoring world hunger, but also equally ignored world hunger and the dog's hunger? The people working at the bakery who thought only about the clientele and the mess made by the dog? The taxi driver, who refused to help the dog, or the bakery cashier, who alleged that she was the owner of the dog, but left it wandering about, abandoned and hungry?

We need to reflect profoundly about this. Could it be that the Adam-like species does not require repair and maintenance? Could it be that we do not need a leader for this project, who can influence actors and participants with the aim of creating a new pattern?

Negative marketing is easy. Positive marketing is for few. Reaching the Promised Land was put off due to negative marketing. There was an occasion on which God ordered that a representative from every tribe of Israel be sent to Canaan in order to define the logistics for the great migration of nearly three million inhabitants to this land. The representatives had to verify the region's geography, observe farming opportunities, plan the best routes, check the inhabitants of the region, and study the enemy's military might.

The chosen men were considered the crème de la crème of society. The best, the most prepared, the fair, the *tzadikim*, bestowed with motivation and leading the people on a journey of victory and full confidence in God's projects. It was their responsibility to describe and show the fruits of this land. They carried out with the mission that was bestowed upon them. However, when the spies returned instead of exposing to the people their lack of faith and weaknesses, they should have talked about confidence in the victory that was God's promise. Their insecurity was reflected in a depreciative report. They were so emphatic about pointing out the obstacles that they contaminated the people with their insecurity. Pessimism contaminates, and it is a disease that spreads like a highly contagious epidemic.

When we concentrate on the obstacle and not on God's action, we do indeed have a big problem. In their case, the big problem was not the obstacles found, but rather the negativist posture that implied unbelief. It is not problems that make us sad and depressed, but rather our attitude toward them. Our attitude is crucial. The war is bothersome and uncomfortable. The spies fled from confrontation because they were still bound by the chains of slavery; their attitudes implied low self-esteem and defeatism. The lack of faith distanced them from the Promised Land and, consequently, from God.

The spies still carried open wounds on their backs, caused by the whips of the oppressive Egyptians. Even so, they preferred the dungeon to having to face a new giant, the unknown Canaanite people who inhabited forts in the Promised Land.

Fear, our old acquaintance is inside our promised land, inhabiting our lives, hindering our full achievement.

Everything you feed will grow: a puppy, a baby, and even fear. Imaginary fears multiply and lead us to overestimate them.

The fear of Egypt was a controlled fear, since it was not unknown. The fear of the Canaanite people was a gigantic, uncontrolled fear, one capable of multiplying the size of the enemy, its force, and its weapons.

To get out of prison, it is necessary that someone from outside participate. It may be a companion who helps with the escape; it may be the jailer who distracts the guard or deliberately causes the escape, it may be a court decision that issues a release order. It is necessary to obtain outside help for both spiritual and psychological prison. To leave the darkness, it is necessary for someone to bring the light, someone who has light. And it is also necessary for the one living in darkness to want to see this light.

Fear made the Canaanites falsify the truth and proclaim defeat, as if there were ten Goliaths mocking God's words. The consequences were destructive, since the frightened people prefer to return to slavery instead of accepting the challenge of reaching the Promised Land.

The slavery of fear tightened the chains, handcuffed and immobilized the people of Israel who in their majority were still prisoners of their past.

The spies were prepared. Much to the contrary, they constituted an elite force and were the distinguished leaders of their tribes. Social pressure caused them to be influenced by the majority, in a search for acceptance.

Only two spies had a mind that was renewed and full of faith. Caleb and Joshua were the only ones who really believed in God's promises. In a simple mathematical sample, using only a simple rule of three, only 16% of the spies had faith. They were sure. They had no doubts.

This statistical quotient shows that really only very few are willing to face challenges with the certainty that God is in command of the operation.

When the macaroni is not the instant kind, it is necessary to find its cooking point. You cook it and then check by biting it. If it does not stick to your teeth, or is too hard, that is because it is not ready! This was the way it was with Israel. The people were not ready. They had not yet recovered from their walk through the desert. The consequence of this negative marketing was 40 years in the desert and a generation that did not have the privilege of enjoying Canaan.

What differentiated Joshua and Caleb from a losing generation was persistence. Giving up cannot be part of our life. Joshua and Caleb were not afraid of those who gave up, but rather had the faith of the perseverant. They were at the perfect cooking point!

We cannot reach the end of our lives saying:

> ***I was almost happy. I almost achieved my goals. At least I left Egypt and got close to the Promised Land …***

This is not consolation, but rather a message of defeat. A person who almost won is someone who lost. It does not matter if he or she lost 100 times or one time, the fact of having lost does not change. Losing in the first or last round makes little difference.

God never gives up on a project or a person. Giving up is emotional weakness; it is lack of faith.

There is a passage in the Bible that describes the saga of four disciples of Yeshua. Fisherman, who lived with their nets in their hands, torn nets full of algae, dirt, etc. There were four partners of the failed and nearly bankrupt "Galilee Fish PLC." The company was not doing so well, because its shareholders, Peter, John, James, and Andrew, gave up when faced with difficulties.

Yeshua found them when they had already landed, when they had already given up fishing. Perseverance demands emotional maturity and faith. Of course there are difficulties, but Yeshua was not looking for four sailors. He was looking for four men prepared for life.

Yeshua asked Peter if he could borrow his boat, the one that had faced a great storm and returned empty to serve as a channel of life and power.

Yeshua filled that boat with his presence and his word. Those fishermen were sad, anguished, and nearly left without hope. Yeshua looked into the depths of the Sea of Galilee and saw that there were giant shoals there. At the same time he looked into the depths of the hearts of his advisors and saw that they were destroyed, despondent, and unmotivated.

Yeshua, a carpenter who understood nothing about boats and fish, ordered the fishermen to cast their nets. Peter's response was not a lamentation, but rather a word from one who was already standing, looking into the sea and at the boat differently, with the nets ready in his hands. Peter said:

> ***Rabbi, we have been working hard the whole night and have caught nothing, but if you say so, we will cast the nets.***

Something incredible happened! The catch was so extraordinary that it nearly sank the boat. It was necessary to call in another vessel, since the result surpassed all expectations.

***

One differential about Yeshua is his innate authority, perceived by all, which brought legitimacy to his teachings.

People did not dare contest him. His speeches were molded within the dimension of his interpreters' capacity for assimilation, since he was a specialist in allegoric speech—

what Judaism understands as Drash. His teachings are quite clear, using examples from daily life to clarify and illustrate his thoughts. Imitating Yeshua involves the adoption of a model that certainly brings us closer to God's expectations.

This rabbi is the model. However, he extrapolates this function, since his authority generates transformations in the lives of those who assimilate his teachings. His weapon was his words. And words can save a life. In fact, the word of God was compared to the most effective weapon of the Roman legions—the sword, the gladius, a short, swift, and lightweight sword that punctured and made the legions faster. This sword is what gave the gladiators their name. A double-edged sword cuts at both ends, since it saves, defends, and attacks. It penetrates, cuts, and divides.

Religion is concerned about the type of hair, the right clothing, painted fingernails or inserts, wigs, length of skirts, what is considered inappropriate on TV, the arts, and the cinema. To summarize, it takes care of the outer part.

However, the word of God takes care of our interior and cuts like a sword, surgically removing what must be extracted from our insides. A major differential in Jesus' life was the authority that he naturally (or supernaturally) carried. He truly practiced what he preached. His words were 100% coherent with his attitude, which brought him credibility. The truth was not only the rhetoric of language, but it was stamped across his face and backed by his attitude.

Credibility is what the world lacks in a general sense. Our authority is associated with our capacity to be sincere. If we really say what we think, if our words in public are the same as our intimate and internal feelings, and if we have the same peripheral discussion with the people with whom we have direct relationships, in whom we bestow the utmost trust, then the sincerity of our interior reflects a coherence that licenses us to plead with the power that comes from God.

Authority and sincerity were keys to the magnetism that enchanted the crowds. And they continue to be enchanting today. Having power does not necessarily mean having authority.

In a simple example from our daily life, take how a boss has the power to fire an employee, but he does not have the authority to make him or her perform a certain task.

Regardless of the amount of authority we have, we are always subordinate to someone. However, the *carte blanche* has its limits even for sovereigns.

The sovereignty of whoever has power is directly associated with his or her definition of conduct, character, and sense of justice. Because nothing comes for free, major powers bring with them major responsibilities.

Certainly, from whoever is given much, much will be expected. It is important for us to perceive that God does not sponsor the political projects of men. His most legitimate representatives cannot become the political canvassers and spokespersons for candidates who want to use faith to leverage support and votes.

In the same way that a baker, in theory, should not sell his bread by placing a banner at the bakery entrance that says:

> ***Buy my croissant, my buns and my sweet rolls because I believe in God's word and that is why I am better than the impious baker on the corner.***

An ethical dentist would never place a billboard in front of his clinic, stating:

> ***Do your root canal with me because I believe in God All-Mighty and I am very religious!***

Yeshua clearly said that his kingdom was found in another world. He did not come to take up arms, spark a revolution, speak during the free political advertisement slot, or to be crowned as a political leader. He did not have horses, carriages, a court, or opportunists and flatterers with him.

He came as *korban* and *cohen gadol* simultaneously. *Korban* is the sacrifice that connects us and brings us closer to the Creator, and *cohen gadol* is the utmost priest, he who intercedes and operates the mechanism of approximation and reconnection. He unites the antagonistic functions and performs them, because this is the role of the REST FACTOR. That is why he died for a cause. He was not the martyr of a revolutionary political project organized into guerillas and using military techniques. He died because this was the purpose from God. This was the great revolution, which many still find difficult to understand.

Human choices are as surprising as they are incorrect. Two thousand years ago, there was a vote. It does not matter what was at stake, but rather the choice that was made. The candidates: Yeshua and Barabbas. Barabbas had a sweeping victory during the first round of the election. If this vote had been made today, I can safely say that Yeshua would lose to Barabbas once again, and by an even larger margin. Yeshua is king by decision and prerogative of God, as opposed to by the vote of men, who normally choose wrong.

Let us not confuse those elected by God with those elected by man, since we have a treacherous heart, a heart that has a hard time discerning, and a heart that is the essence of the "homo-stupidus."

Another characteristic in Yeshua's behavior is that he spoke with confidence and determination. He did not see his neighbor as a threat. His power respected free will. His power for curing and releasing others respected peoples' freedom. The sick only seek out a doctor when they identify or recognize the disease. If they consider this to be normal, they do not seek medication or treatment.

Every lesson of Yeshua can be summarized by charity and humility, or in other words, the two virtues that are the opposite of selfishness and pride. Humility and charity are characteristics that he recommends, providing the example in his own behavior. Pride and selfishness are characteristics that he does not cease fighting. He does not only recommend charity, he explicitly emphasizes it as the absolute condition for achieving future happiness.

What is curious and thought provoking is the authority of one of the most well known followers of Yeshua, the Rabbi Paul, when he said:

Imitate me, as I'm of the mashiach.

By making this affirmation, he names himself as a model. A model inspired in the main model, but which still proposes to be a standard. This declaration, in principle, might seem an expression of presumption and arrogance, but Paul, one of the most efficient followers of the *mashiach*, had a deep rupture of values, changed his concepts, and developed a spiritual IQ to the point of becoming committed to his convictions so much that he would die for them.

Could it be that someone, with our credentials, would be able to make such an affirmation? Even if this question was provocative and required some lengthy reflection, the truth is that we have a very serious problem. If we do not imitate the messiah, then who will we imitate?

We have desires and fears, tastes and longings, and all of these passions express our nature and reflect that which we are. It is our desires that drive us and determine our choices, risks, and paths. Life is a reflection of all of this; we are a mirror reflecting our desires. Our identity is built upon our interests.

Desire is not limited to need. It involves appetites, varied intensities and is subject to changes; it is a passion.

From the economic point of view, scarcity is defined not as absence, but as an eternal state of desire to consume. The more socially excluded a person is, the greater his or her desire to use fantasies. An adolescent who spends all the money he earned from his first job buying electronic gadgets, designer label clothing, and tennis shoes that are often worth more than twice his salary, or a woman who feels better buying designer label purses and shoes, or a young yuppie who works in the financial market and buys a fancy car to increase his status—they all have the same symptom: "fetish for merchandise."

Our society makes us think that we consume objects, but what we really seek are the ideals behind the objects. We do not buy items based on their usefulness, but rather to guarantee some sense to our existence. Our appetite is not for consumer goods, but for the prestige and power camouflaged behind these objects.

The appetite of Rabbi Saul, also known as Paul of Tarsus, was something else. For him, being is more important than possessing. When addressing the issue of imitating the Messiah, he committed himself to disseminating the image and resemblance of God, since by inspiring him on what was really the best example of the image and resemblance of divine nature, he also positioned himself in alignment with this principle.

Paul's path was quite curious. Although he was renewed, he was also a man who assumed his role of a model in the past, tied to the religious system (every religious system is dogmatic and exclusivist); he was the model of intolerance and persecution. His role as an active member of the Sanhedrin was to persecute and report the Jews who followed the Messiah Yeshua. His religious background was outstanding. He was an obstinate, intense man of great conviction. He persecuted Yeshua because he believed that heresies should not exist among the people.

He was raised at the feet of Gamaliel, a renowned rabbi, grandson of Hillel, one of the greatest rabbis of all time who inspired countless followers. Because they had different interpretations of the Torah, the Rabbis Hillel and Shammai founded two distinct schools of thought.

God must have seen the energy and potential of Paul, and after thinking it over, he must have said: I cannot lose a guy like this. Paul was transformed into a new model. There was a factory recall, he replaced the parts and changed the course of his history.

We were created to reflect God's image. And this helps us review our own identity.

What about us? What is our essence? What character do we represent? Could it be that we are coherent and always play the same role? Are we a model? Are we the employee of the month who has his or her photos displayed on the wall of a fast food restaurant?

Certainly, we are more condescending with our children than we are with our parents, since we tend to be impatient with those who give us life, and subconsciously we want to teach them, while we actually could learn a lot from them.

We assume the role of tough skinned people who are self-sufficient at work, where we try not to appear insecure, but at home with our wives we melt like ice cream and show our fragility when under pressure.

We assume the role of comedians and well-humored merrymakers with our closest friends, but we assume the role of inaccessible grouches when we relate to employees or people in a professional position who are hierarchically inferior.

We appear controlled and patient when our children throw tantrums in the shopping mall, but as soon as we get in the car, a wave of anger washes over us, without the presence of the judging eye of elements foreign to family living, and we explode and yell at them, leaving our discontent clear.

We laugh and show our teeth to some and hide our sense of civility from others. We have variable and fluctuating behavior based on our interests. However, we have more than two faces; we actually have infinite faces, as if we represent different characters during the day. We wear masks based on our own convenience.

We do not serve as a model because we are mutants and we are not concerned about coherence of values.

I invite you to reflect and think about something: Since we are not the best reference, what type of reference do people have of you? How do people around you refer to you?

Is your mouth a source of drinkable or contaminated water? Could it be that the words that leave your mouth have a flavor similar to the sophisticated bottles of French mineral water, but we insist on serving them in a dirty cup? Everything we say is heard and analyzed by other people. If we only use our mouths to complain or groan, we will certainly be seen as moody, cranky, and ill tempered. If we spend all of our time saying silly things, we will not be taken seriously, and others will think that we are childish and not very reliable. If our vocabulary is brimming with bad words, we will be seen as people in need of fixing, and if we insist on this, we will be considered a negative reference.

Who do you want to be for the people around you? Just another face in the crowd? Do you want to catch the attention of others by being the class clown, the compulsive showoff at the office, the one who makes fun of situations? Do you want to be known as the guy who is always bad-tempered? The potty-mouth? Or do you want to be the person who makes a difference, the one in whom others can trust, the one who they can ask for advice, the person that always has a cheerful word?

The choice is yours!

Thus, if we do not contribute to transforming the world, we contribute to making it worse.

***

A kingdom is an organization that can be defined as a state. The State is an institution organized politically, socially, and legally, which occupies a defined territory, where the highest law is a constitution written and directed by a ruler, in this case, a king.

A king needs subjects; he needs citizens. The concession of citizenship to the *malchut* (kingdom) of God must be obtained through the process of *teshuvah* (repentance). We must understand this concept, its dimension, and its implications on our life and our behavior.

The *Tikkun Olam* is the project planned by God, and Yeshua is the operational leader of this project. Its objective consists of treating the imperfections of the Adam-like species, creating a process of spiritual inclusion, also known as salvation.

No process occurs with a snap of the fingers. The only thing that is ready in three minutes is instant noodles. The improvement process is similar to a rally, where there are control posts at different stages, with methods for calculating the results and metrics defined.

This process can be anticipated in our lives before it is established in the world, and accordingly, we can claim the benefits of this relationship before the scheduled time, obtaining a full shalom.

In other words, when the *malchut* is established in our hearts, our passport will be duly stamped for the new frontiers of spiritual inclusion.

CHAPTER 8

UNLOCKING THE LANGUAGE

When he wants to reveal himself, God speaks to us through the only language we understand—the language of suffering. This is the base of communication, because we are essentially monolingual. We dominate French, English, Portuguese, Spanish, etc. but the raw reality is that when it comes to understanding God, we are limited to "the language of suffering." Most times, he does not speak to us like the he spoke to the prophet Samuel—who heard him audibly—but rather through his spirit, filling our interior with certainties and convictions so truly absolute that they turn our heart into a universal recipient for his language. Therefore, pain indicates an attempt at communication. In a stunningly beautiful poem, poet Carlos Drummond de Andrade wrote:

> ***Every day that I live, the more convinced I am that we waste our lives on the love we do not give, on the efforts we do not make, on the egotistical prudence that risks nothing, and that, sparing ourselves from suffering, we also lose our happiness. Pain is inevitable. Suffering is optional.***

And he was right, pain is sometimes quite good for us, it is great therapy. It is not lethal nor does it do us as much harm as we think.

Pain is excellent ground for growth. It is quite fertile ground. The desert is God's great laboratory, where his methods are applied to correct and trim the edges of our character traits. The desert is God's great incubator. We go there to receive doses of his medicine and to produce antibodies. Those things that seem to be bad are not always truly so.

There is a remedy. God says that he is near the downcast and those who seek him are in a fragile and dependent state. In religious language, this is called feebleness. It would be metaphorically comparable to a hypothetical heart surgery, in which the surgeon removes the heart from the rib cage and then places the organ in the blender to cut it into countless pieces. This is the heart transplant that works. It is not enough to raise the white flag, capitulate intellectually and show this symbolically. There must also be a modified spirit that makes it possible to dominate and tame pride and passions, which will enable us to accept the will of the God, joyfully and without resistance.

The subjugated will, represented by the hoisting of the white flag and a feeble spirit are not the same thing. Will is found in intellect, while the spirit is found within the sphere of the heart.

God has style and knows how to impress his people. On Mount Sinai, with thunder and lightning, Israel came face to face with the power of God, declaring in unison:

Nasseh VeNishmah (We will do and we will hear).

This was the "yes" of a marriage. It was the formalization of an alliance. Contrary to the tragic ending of Romeo and Juliet, in a story brimming with conflicts between the Capulets and Montagues, on Mount Sinai a true love story took place.

This marriage began with all due care, with affection and respect. In this relationship the bride got to know the groom gradually. The groom revealed his essence little by little. God invited the bride to go out into the desert and prepared a different path there. In the desert they were alone. There was no noise, no outside interference, no lack of attention.

Free from all confusion, in the silence of an arid region, although one rich in dialogue, the groom courted the bride. The bride began to see the groom's character; she treated him with respect and admiration. Intimacy developed between them. Through the words *Nasse VeNishmah* the people of Israel expressed their readiness to serve God, out of their free will and with absolute devotion. They promised to unconditionally adopt the Divine Laws, as the basis of their entire existence, sealing an eternal pact with God.

Alliances rely on signatories. The invitation was made, the bride accepted the role of protagonist, and she took the initiative to seal the pact and finally made the alliance official.

The marriage goes through crises—all marriages do.

Time shows this. When the honeymoon ended, the thirst quenched and the hunger satisfied. Men –whose permanent natural state is dissatisfaction—began to grumble and complain about God. There was a dissonance between the will and spirit of men, since even though they had stated, "We will do it," there was no true feebleness.

God knows us. We cannot surprise him, and only he has the right to dig into the depths of our being, sweep our interior, and examine our essence.

That is why there is truly a mystery in suffering. It is through suffering that we gain the strength to look at God, to discover his essence and feel his presence.

It is important that we understand that pain exists to strengthen us permanently and penetrate our understanding properly.

The logic from God is the opposite of humanist logic, which bestows upon man resources and possibilities. It is in a state of weakness, associated with the understanding of dependence on God that the remedy works. It is when we are weak that we are prepared to receive the strength that comes from him. The history of the Exodus from Egypt is a passage celebrated religiously by Jewish people during the *Pesach* ceremony. This festive ritual is described in the *Pesach's Haggadah*, which includes scriptural passages, prayers, and songs associated with the occasion. This period reports that the people who were in Egypt experienced a great torment but grew and multiplied until the moment that finally culminated in their liberation. God himself said to Moses in a biblical passage:

> ***I have seen the affliction of my people, I have heard their clamor.***

God does not only declare to have knowledge of the people's suffering, but he also describes this suffering. We can be sure that he knows and has seen all of our afflictions, and that at the right moment, he will free us from our anguish and lead us to the Promised Land. He knows every one of your sufferings in detail, because in his immensity there is nothing too small. Those who minimize his importance and think that their problems and suffering are not of interest of the Eternal because they are not important enough, actually believe in a God who is much smaller and weaker than what he really is. Perhaps these people are looking for a way out of avoiding fully surrendering to him.

Nobody is immune to pain and suffering. Nobody, absolutely nobody, not even the wisest or richest person, will be able to go through life without experiencing problems.

It is a mistake to believe that the great, opulent, distinct, and well-structured families, such as those of the 19th century, who posed for old black and white photos, had no problems or afflictions. We also get confused with television commercials in which beautiful models who represent perfect couples and parents of healthy, rosy-cheeked children happily eat their breakfast cereal and drink fruit juice or skimmed milk in perfect harmony. They represent a society in which people live carefree, easy lives in which there are no problems or concerns, but this world only exists in the universe of publicity and advertising.

Not all problems in life are big, but all are important within the process designed by God to mold our character.

When he told Abraham to gather his belongings and hit the road, he did not immediately reveal where he was taking him. Abraham was an authentic "easyrider" on a Route 66 that did not exist. But there was a purpose to this journey: change through the revelation of God's word.

Abraham was literally kicked out of his home. There is a passage in the Torah that uses the term *Lech Lecha*, which in Hebrew means: "Go, for you," whose context is associated with the idea of "for your own benefit."

In the story of Abraham's departure from his native city, the instruction from God sounded like a warning from an official of justice, ordering him to abandon his parents, his place of birth, and his father's house. It is the abandonment of all influence. If we are hostages of the influence of the world around us, what is the purpose of our creation? The cooking time in the pressure pot catalyzes the metabolism process of the chemical reactions necessary to destroy all traces of self-sufficiency that exist in our lives. The food becomes more tasty, less acidic, smoother, and has a better seasoning. The consistency changes, the flavor changes, and the spiritual IQ acquired during the cooking process allow us to influence and not be influenced by strange flavors. The cooking time is crucial for defining the specific flavor we need to have.

The seasoning only penetrates and gives flavor to our life during the pressure pot period. Salt, cumin, basil, cinnamon, hot pepper, nutmeg, and the countless spices of the earth, work well during the cooking time. It is our duty to leave our mark in this world—to season it. This is a challenge that we must accept. We have to influence and contribute to improvement, not to the manipulation of people. Manipulating is when one person influences us with the purpose of obtaining personal gain, while influencing is for another's benefit.

I was once asked what profession I would choose for my son (he was 13 at the time). At first I thought that the question was quite funny since it did not make much sense to me and my child would be able to freely choose whatever he wanted to do. However, after I thought it over calmly, I realized that the question made sense, since after all, if I do not influence my child, another person will, and nobody knows him better than I do. I cannot fail to exercise my paternity.

God did not fail to appear to Abraham. The message of *Lech Lecha* is not something associated with a concept of departure, but rather arrival. It is the birth of awareness, awakening, in which the young Abraham leaves the cocoon, opens his wings and becomes the mature Abraham. It is a metamorphosis and a personal journey that speaks of change. Not the change made by a transporter that boxes and packages our personal belongings during a merely geographical journey, but something much more substantial.

Moses also had his *Lech Lecha*. God also asked for change. And during this meeting with God, Moses said: "*Hineni*"—"Here I am here" (the same answer that Abraham gave God when asked to sacrifice Isaac). The Eternal revealed himself as God of the father of Moses, Abraham, Isaac, and Jacob. He then explained his plan to remove the people from Egypt and take them to a land of milk and honey. Then he sent Moses to the Pharaoh.

What is interesting is that God is identified by the name of those who serve, respect, and obey him. This shows how our way of acting is fundamental, and this is of utmost importance in our relationship with God, since it is one of the main aspects that defines our essence and affects the way that God sees us.

This is also commonly called "witness," since it expresses in our attitude the values we have to change the world around us.

We can imagine the possibility of God presenting himself to us one day, using a mechanism common to the modern businessmen, delivering a business card that reads: ***I am the God of "A," "B," or "C."***

The truth is that we need to better understand that we are God's business card; he builds relationships with men. When he appeared before Moses, he identified himself as God of the patriarchs Abraham, Isaac, and Jacob, confirming that he is committed to those who are committed to him. God's reciprocity is built upon alliances.

's journey could not stop. The caravan took many people, but not all went all the way. Some stopped in Haran in the middle of the path, like Terah, father of Abraham. Terah acted like we do. He headed out toward a certain place, but settled in another along the way. He became disheartened and tired. He lacked patience, desire, and perseverance. The excitement did not last long. New ventures and initiatives can be stimulating simply due to their novelty. Excitement will carry a person for a while, but it will not carry him or her to the destination. Responsibility and commitment are also necessary.

Personal responsibility cannot be delegated because it is something that comes from within one's being. Commitment, responsibility, and faith are non-separable. They do not exist apart. They need maturity. A baby does not have any responsibility, but as he grows, it is expected that he will assume more and more responsibilities. God's teachings follow the same principle.

And why do we go through ordeals?

The moments of great pain in our lives reflect the exact instant at which God proves our faith and polishes our character.

What we say to God during moments of joy expresses gratitude, but what we say on days of anguish expresses our faith and confidence. It is on the day of tribulation that our character truly shows, since we are exposed and nude. This is when we should remove the stiff-necked collar that hinders us from reducing our levels of pride, arrogance, and self-sufficiency to humble ourselves in the eyes of God.

The obstacles that appear in our lives can be compared to tests during the school year. Educational evaluations show how much teaching has been absorbed and understood; God's tests reveal the level of learning that we have achieved.

We will be tempted and tested precisely where we are weak. The truth is that we do not want to go through the ordeals in our life. We want to take shortcuts in the middle of the path.

God has not always guided us along the path that we presume to be the path of happiness. Like the people of Israel, although our goal is nearby, we frequently have to make detours before entering the Promised Land. Just as he did with this people, God, seeing that we are not prepared for discipline and obedience, guides us in the opposite direction until we reach what he expects of us.

We always expect a straight line between ourselves and the desire of our heart, but we are disappointed to see that, for God, things do not work this way. It was he who said in Isaiah:

> ***For my thoughts are not your thoughts, neither are your ways my ways.***

The paths of God are higher, different than ours, because his perspective and objectives are different. We want to be happy at any price, exactly like the people of Israel wanted bread, meat, and water. We even have ridiculous needs. However, the power that comes from God is generous. It helps us grow as we develop our spiritual IQ and strengthen our relationship with him.

Our vision is microscopic and limited by time. God's vision is eternal and he wants to prepare us for something bigger and more lasting. Those who have been in the pressure pot did not stay in a five-star hotel. Rather, they had an interesting and unique opportunity. It is precisely in this "period of incubation and cooking" that we get the grandiose opportunity to change our flavor, getting closer to the recipe prepared by God.

Miracles do not transform our character. The path to certain liberations involves extremely difficult proof. When we are treated by God, the handcuffs and chains begin to break and a real truth sets us free. The major issue is not beating our demons, but rather allowing God to win us over.

Miracles work like a gas station and convenience store in the middle of the desert. Miracles are a 21st century version oasis, but you will soon see a sign that will always indicate that there is a residual mileage to be covered to reach the promised land.

We have to suffer ordeals in order for our character to be molded. Sometimes we are equipped in the areas where we dedicate a greater focus of attention, such as in the case of Abraham, who was ordered to sacrifice his own son. If Yeshua did not escape this process and we are better than him in no way, then each of us has the duty to travel through the desert.

There is no way out. Sooner or later that inevitable moment will come in which God will implode the pillars of our self-sufficiency with mighty sticks of dynamite. When we are rowing against the tide and currents, the wisest attitude is to let go of the oars, raise the sail and let the wind blow.

This is not accommodation, since the very best sailors are those who respect the winds and care for the boat. This is spiritual IQ. Regardless of how much our words and chants say something different, we think we know more than God about what we really need. We run over God's will. The result is always the same: tragedy.

It is man in his eternal existential conflict: self-sufficiency vs. help from God

Imagine Jacob in hypothetical psychological treatment during the time of his turbulent conflict with Esau. And what if he searched within himself and only within himself for the strength to overcome his adversities? What if he sought his strength in self-confidence as opposed to confidence in God, if he searched for excessive self-worth, when the truth is that he was ripped apart and hurt inside? What if he sought self-analysis, when his sense of reason was destroyed, and if he sought self-help, when he was not even apt to receive help? The result of this all would have been a serious existential crisis!

I believe that, after the therapist had made his diagnosis, the cure would have been based on transfer. It would be necessary to find a culprit. The therapist could have told Jacob that his problems stemmed from a childhood trauma, from rejection by his father, who openly preferred his brother Esau. The psychologist would address the Oedipus complex issue due to his relationship with Rebecca and would identify the gigantic inferiority complex developed due to the skills of the hunter Esau, a shadow that Jacob would carry forever. In other words, several sessions of therapy would be necessary for Jacob to treat his problems: he fought with his brother in the uterus, he was nearly kicked out of his home without a cent to his name, he was led to marry a woman he did not love, he had a father-in-law who wanted to kill him, his only daughter was raped, his children took revenge by assassinating an entire town, his beloved died during childbirth, and everything culminated with the sale of his son Joseph into slavery, betrayed by his brothers.

Therapy would have taken years and he probably would have never confronted the Angel. He would not be Israel. He would not have transformed; he would not have renewed his mind. His desert would be endless, and it would be a giant labyrinth.

The renewal of the mind means a new perspective on life. It means a lesson, something new, a new moral and intellectual birth.

The seventeenth-century English philosopher John Locke, considered one of the fathers of Empiricism, created the theory of *Tabula Rasa* (literally meaning white marble), and less literally, "clean slate." According to Locke none of us know anything at birth. We bring no impressions or any knowledge with us into the world. The entire process of understanding, knowing, and acting is learned through experience, through trial and error. And it is precisely in youth that we are best able to assimilate knowledge. It is a phase of discoveries and the quick assimilation of knowledge.

We study in our youth, when the mind is alert, malleable, and absorbent, when our sharp memory will accept and retain what we study just like new paper retains ink, remaining vivid and lasting. Older age sometimes hinders and weakens concentration.

Teaching a mind filled with its own experiences, with certainties constructed during the life process, and conceptions built up during the course of an existence, forces us to eliminate old concepts before learning new ones. To summarize, it is like writing on paper that is already full of writing—we must erase the old ink. Otherwise, the paper will become smudgy and the new ink will run.

This is a concept of Rabbi Elisha Ben Abuiah, who wrote about the *Mishnah* in the compendium known as *Pirkei Avot* (Ethics of our Fathers).

The Torah can be compared to the ink, which only has an effect on our lives when there is new, clean paper inside us. The ink is the means for making marks on the paper. It serves to transmit thoughts and ideas. It only transforms if the reception is good.

If the page is dirty and inappropriate for use, the solution is to turn it over, use a new one, and begin again.

Yeshua understood this very well. He speaks about it, about renewal, and a new perspective:

> ***So children were brought to him so that he could put his hands on them and pray for them, but the disciples scolded the people who brought them. However, Yeshua said: "Let the children come to me and do not stop them; because he who does not welcome the Kingdom of God like a child shall not enter."***

This passage does not only refer to real children, but also to those who still live inside adults.

Give me the purity, innocence, pleasure, and joy of living that still can be found hidden in this adult body, adulterated by its values. Let your child come forward, the one not contaminated by your adult, with full faith, not so intellectualized that it blocks your purity. We need our mind to be a *Tabula Rasa*.

There is nothing more volatile than writing on the sand or earth, where the wind and water wash the writing away. Yeshua wrote personal messages on the sand in such a way that only those interested could read them. Those who are interested make the effort. Do not depend only on old, used pages. Be open to a renewal that helps you face and overcome obstacles.

CHAPTER 9

EXPOSING PRIDE

Pride and beliefs of the past impede us from accepting the teachings of those whose paths and thoughts are infinitely HIGHER than ours.

Our ego corresponds to an unreal, idealized, and artificial image that we build of ourselves. Because it is very inflated, it becomes fragile and thin like a soap bubble. Whenever it bursts, it brings us back down to reality, forcing us to put our feet on the ground. There are people who see themselves to be so superior and special that they believe that all things must be done according to their will.

Pride reveals itself to be an exaggerated perception of one's self. Our exaggerated "I" requires pomp and ceremony that does not correspond to our essence.

Pride numbs us, creating the illusion that we are extremely important, comparable to a light gas in a balloon. It is as if there were a device pumping hydrogen inside a balloon called ego, which has a small hole, nearly undetectable to the naked eye. As we fill it with more gas, the balloon called ego inflates, and the small hole gets bigger and expands.

At a given moment, pride, which generates the inflated ego, is the harbinger of a great tragedy. Pride precedes destruction. The small hole pops the balloon and it falls abruptly to the ground. This pride, which distances us from reality, is present in all human beings to one degree or another. Certain balloons have little hydrogen, but others are dangerously inflated.

It is always very difficult to see pride within us; it is much easier to see it in others.

Pride prevents us from being who we really are; it prevents us from finding our true "I."

Pride distorts reality because it is an illusion. When someone is a prisoner of pride, he or she separates him or herself from others, since the inflated balloon flies very high and people seen from it appear tiny.

***

In the Bible, we find the record of the attitude of a man with leprosy whose name was Naaman and who went to Israel to be cured and have a meeting with God. However, the story is not quite that simple.

During a Syrian raid on Israel, a girl was taken captive and placed at the service of Naaman's wife. As soon as she got used to her new home, God's purpose revealed the motive behind her capture. She suggested to her mistress that her husband's illness could be cured if she met with the prophet Elisha.

One of the most picturesque stories on the instruction that comes from God is revealed. During a succession of events, sovereign Syria sends its five-star general to Israel in order to meet with its king. However, Naaman ends up stopping right in front of the doors of the prophet Elisha who, impressed with the presence of the general and his army, did not receive him, but rather told him to go to the River of Jordan for a purification wash. This could have become a serious diplomatic incident. When he sought out the Prophet Elisha, the latter sent him a message telling him to wash himself seven times in the River of Jordan. Naaman was indignant about the fact that he was not received with all due pomp. Naaman was also upset with the instruction to wash himself in the River of Jordan, since, according to him, his land had better rivers than the Jordan.

It was not easy for Naaman to follow Elisha's advice. It was actually God who was inviting the general to find humility, feebleness, and fully surrender himself to God's authority.

Happily for Naaman, his officers convinced him to try out the prescription given by Elisha. This was his salvation. He washed himself based on the instructions and was cured. Obviously, he was extremely embarrassed. After all, it was not easy to expose himself before the troop completely naked, with sores and degenerative wounds indicating a disease that was incurable at the time and he was cured not only of the disease of leprosy, but primarily of the disease of pride.

Nobody likes to be exposed in public. It may be that our shame does not have the same dimension as that of Naaman, but we certainly have something to wash away in the river.

Everyone has some dirty clothing to wash. In the past, people washed themselves in rivers and streams. They did so side-by-side, neighbors and friends.

Because we live in a society where everyone is dressed, inevitably one day all of us will have to wash our clothes. And of course, dirty clothes bother others because they smell bad. This gave rise to the expression: Wash your dirty clothes at home. Nobody wants to wash them in public; the exposure scares us. It is pride, camouflaging and impeding transformation, cleaning, and purification.

Humiliation and shame are two sides of the same coin. And if the coin had three sides, pride would appear with a big smile. We can "destroy" a person, needing only to harm his or her personal dignity in front of a group. The "art" of ridicule begins with depreciative comments, continues with verbal aggression and ends in insults. The process is always an attempt to incite shame.

When we feel humbled, the first sensation that comes to mind is to hide; it is to hide our faces; we seek solitude, a place to be alone, where we cannot be seen.

Humiliation comes from the recognition of our own state, of our weaknesses and defects. Humiliation is a state of shame and impotence. However, paradoxically humiliation before God is a benefit. Man's humiliation before God is the foundation of prayer. Humiliation is a necessity, because in this way, the pride and grandeur of man are eliminated.

> ***If my people, who call me by my name, humble themselves and pray, and look for my face and cease from their evil ways, then I shall hear from the heavens and forgive their sins, and heal their earth.***

The state of humiliation before God does not give him any type of pleasure. Certainly, humiliation does not please anyone, and neither can it be pleasant for God. However, it exists and is necessary to allow man to recognize his real situation and, therefore, be able to perceive his relationship of dependence.

Is it possible to measure humiliation? What is the size of your humiliation? Understand that this depends on the size of your ego, since feeling ridiculed and humiliated is to attribute excessive value to society's opinion.

Why do you feel humiliated? Humiliated because your name has dirty credit? Humiliated because your team lost? Humiliated because the person you love ridiculed you? Humiliated because you live off favors? Humiliated at school because your friends make mean jokes?

The size of humiliation is directly proportional to the size of our pride.

Naaman truly lived a drama. He lived a dilemma that we also experience. We know that we need to find the answer within ourselves, identifying who we want to serve, either God or our own ego. We need to decide whether or not we will ridicule the instruction from God as idolaters. The worshipping of our personality is the most concrete expression of idolatry that exists within us, as we serve our personal conveniences and our individual interests.

When all of this is clearly defined, when we place God in his due place and occupy our position of true servants, everything becomes easier. The "children of promises" must also learn how to be the "children of obedience."

Theoretically, many sincere people agree without blinking that we are servants of God. However, in practice, people do not always act as such.

The Pharisees and scribes felt superior to the others since they considered themselves to have in-depth knowledge of the Torah.

All of those who had not studied very much, all of those who were humble, all who did not know how to read, all those who required religious orientation belonged to the class of simplest people.

There were, initially, two defined classes: the upper class, which included the scribes, Pharisees, Sadducees and priests, and the low class, consisting of the humblest and all those who did not have much knowledge of the law of God.

However, there was also a third class. There was also the group of publicans (tax collectors) and sinners. Only the most despised people in society belonged to that class, especially thieves and prostitutes, considered pariahs by the public opinion of the time. A religious man called Simon invited the *mashiach* to have dinner with him. Yeshua accepted the invitation, entered the home of the Pharisee and sat down at the table.

A woman of dubious reputation knew about this meeting and decided to go to Simon's home, even though she had not been invited. She went as a "gatecrasher," but took along "a flask of alabaster with perfume."

Yeshua does not exclude people. However, Simon sought to prevent her entering. Our reaction would be no different. We act this way when we do not like someone. We, who are excellent critics, never stop making accusations and condemnations.

However, see how Yeshua reacted: he did not deny that the women had committed several errors, but this did not stop him from interacting with her.

While Simon only saw defects, the *mashiach* saw great sadness in her soul. He could see that she was deeply regretful, willing to abandon the ways of her past. He knew that she no longer wanted to act like she had before.

When he proclaiming the absolution of the woman, the only thing Yeshua considered was the faith she demonstrated with her act of repentance, humiliation, and abnegation.

We judge others based on our metrics, and normally we have more deception than admiration.

Thomas Hobbes, a 16th century English philosopher, spoke about a state of human nature in a book called *Leviathan*. Man is born biologically equal. The sun rises for all. In a society without a state, without political mediation, without the control of power and no imposed order, human nature prevails. Accordingly, each has the right to everything and, once all things are scarce, there is a constant war of all against all—*Bellum omnia omnes*. However, men have a desire, which is also in their own interest, to end war, and that is why they form societies based on a social contract.

Human nature has two vertices: reason and equality. As each individual gains more self-awareness, he or she believes him or herself to be superior, and because man does not desire equality, he seeks to differentiate himself through wealth, glory, and honor. After all, human nature is an eternal state of war. We seek differentiation. Men want inequality against the state of equality, even if they must use violence to attain this.

Man reached the conclusion that a group of individuals acting on behalf of their individuality causes anarchy and promotes disorder. Accordingly, they transfer their freedom to the sovereign, granting him power.

As a result there arises the need for a leader; the need for a "Caesar."

In the year 44 BC, Gaius Julius Caesar was a general greatly loved by the troops. He earned fame for sometimes coming down off his horse and engaging in man-to-man combat if necessary. He led his legionaries onward to memorable victories that expanded the borders of Rome significantly. His campaigns in Gaul, Greece, and Egypt took him far from home for long periods and gave the Roman Republic its golden era. Caesar became famous in Rome, since he "pacified" Gaul (the territory where France is today), which he described as a primitive region even though it was inhabited by people and tribes with a sophisticated and even advanced social structure. Some of the Gauls defeated or "pacified" by Rome had huge sailing ships and controlled the trade routes on the English Channel. Caesar wasted no time and ordered the construction of galleys with battering rams at the tip that were apt for attack but also adapted for the calm Mediterranean Sea. There was fighting, but the price of victory was high. More battles took place on land against the Belgian and Germanic peoples after crossing the Rhine. Rome became Europe's first superpower. The reality, however, was that Caesar had some serious domestic problems, since a few years later after victory over his rival Pompeii, he was assassinated in front of the entire Roman Senate by conspirators, one of whom was his adoptive son, Brutus.

Gaius Julius Caesar was stabbed 23 times and his final words demonstrated above all a heart ripped apart by ingratitude, especially of Brutus, who he considered his only son:

Tu quoque, Brutus, fili mi! (Even you, Brutus, my son!)

A triumvirate formed by the consuls Gaius Julius Caesar Octavius, Mark Anthony, and Marcus Emilius Lepidus, succeeded Caesar. The three fought with each other, but Octavius eventually assumed the power, since he was extremely clever. He proclaimed himself emperor of Rome twenty-seven years before Yeshua and began to use the title of Augustus, which belonged exclusively to the gods of the Roman pantheon. With Octavius, the Rome of bricks became the Rome of marble, engineering, and opulence. Imperial Rome brought Latin and its alphabet to the entire known world.

The *PAX Romana* emerged, which was actually armed PEACE.

The basic line of thinking of human relations is balanced by the concept of order and safety. The "Caesar" should be responsible for safety.

In a certain sense, in the world of today, PEACE reminds us a bit of the time of Imperial Rome. For many thinkers and philosophers, today we have the so-called "*PAX Americana*".

However, if we venture away from an amplified vision of the world and analyze modern regional and urban microcosms, many new facets appear. What is peace in the periphery of major urban metropolises? PEACE is strong police. Armed police repressing disorder.

What is peace in the world? A strong hegemonic state, guaranteeing the status of the free Western world, preserving the "American way of life" against disorderly and barbaric nations. Besides their economic interests, certain current wars aim to preserve this status quo in specific regions.

During the Cold War there were two hegemonic powers (the USSR and the USA) and the fight for PAX occurred through the principle of a balancing of forces. The limits were the subjective continental borders. That is why the Cuban missile crisis was so serious and dangerous for the United States, and the response given was American bases with their missiles pointed at the extinct USSR.

This was the peace of balance, the armed PAX. It is the same "peace" as between two strong adolescents at high school, where both give each other dirty looks, create groups of influence, but avoid direct contact, since they know the consequences. It is human nature, a conflicting nature. A nature that seeks to overcome, that seeks victory, which has its own interests.

There is only life in society when there is domination. Domination only exists when the dominated legitimate or accept their domination. If the legitimacy ends, the domination also ends. Men live seeking domination. Some seek it based on legal aspects, accepting rules, accepting the vote. Traditional domination is exercised through elements of tradition, family, and religious power. According to Max Weber, the state has the monopoly of the use of violence through coercive forces.

War is the expression of domination. War is the most devastating event that exists in the world. You push a button to begin it, but there is no button to make it stop.

There is a war that has not ended. That war began between the son of Hagar (Ishmael) and the son of Sarah (Isaac). A war that has lasted four thousand years, between the child of God's will (promise) and the child of human will, between the child of obedience and the child of independence, a war between the child of self-sufficiency and the child of sufficiency that comes from God.

It may not seem like it, but this challenge still exists in our lives today. It seems so easy to follow the world's rules and accept the paths that others follow. Sometimes, a simple word or small gesture is enough; other times we must simply keep quiet and hold ourselves back. Agreement eliminates conflict.

However, the perspective of living a peaceful life, without any conflict, always having the same position, is a perspective of one who does not want war, of the child of human will.

It is crucial to leave the comfort zone. Conflict exists and it is necessary to follow the path of rupture, following the GPS from God. This path is not comfortable, and no red carpet will be laid down along it. To the contrary, there will be obstacles and lots of rejection.

After World War I, millions of people died and millions of people were mutilated. And the pain and suffering made people think. Within this scenario the League of Nations was created (the predecessor to the UN), and through good will and mutual trust it was believed that an idealistic peace would emerge and that nations would observe the decree of peace through respect for international law.

Less than ten years passed and World War II started. Utopian idealism ended and pragmatic realism began.

Many still ask today: Where is peace in the world? Where is the long awaited world peace?

However, there was an Orthodox rabbi who traveled through Jerusalem and who talked about the *PAX Romana* as it was written in John 14:27:

What I'm leaving with you is shalom—I'm giving you my shalom.
I don't give the way the world gives.

Yeshua speaks about a peace that is not *PAX Romana*.

The Roman Empire completed a mission that it believed to be civilizing and expansionist. This mission was primarily ethnocentric. Rome saw the Hebrew society based on its own cultural parameters. What was not Roman was exotic and inferior.

The *PAX Romana* was the ideology of dominion and armed peace. False peace.

However, in the *Tanakh*, in the book of Isaiah, there is a prophecy about a solid peace in the world, a different shalom.

Could it be that there is a contradiction, seeing that Yeshua has already been in this world and peace is a concept that still does not predominate?

The answer is that peace will not come to those who reject it, but rather to those who want it.

Within any person who believes in Yeshua, there is Shalom. It is not only peace, but health and integrity as well. There is plentitude.

It is not the false peace that ignores the suffering of others, but a lasting peace. Upon his return, Yeshua said: *Shalom Aleichem!* May peace be with us! A very well known passage of Jewish liturgy, in which shalom is not only the absence of conflict, but it brings a concept of peace of mind, security, well-being, health, and success. It is not only peace between two people greeting one another, but it is about something much deeper: plentitude.

So much is said about pacification. Pacifying oneself involves self-knowledge, but it is not only about knowing yourself well and understanding how you work. To achieve this plentitude of peace, "self-knowledge" is necessary.

After all, we have to transfer our freedom to the right monarch. The basis of the social contract explained by the 18th Century Illuminist Swiss philosopher, Jean Jacques Rousseau, is precisely this: the consensual transfer of power. The "Social Contract," by considering that all men are born free and equal, views the state as the object of a contract, in which individuals do not waive their natural rights. Rather, to the contrary, they enter into an agreement to protect these rights. They are rights that the state must preserve, since this is why it is created.

What is even more curious is that the Jewish liturgy points out a basic premise:

Adonai yimloch leolam vaed (God will reign forever).

***

Peace must be desired, understood, and absorbed. The Bible leaves it clear that the function of the Messiah is not decorative; it is not limited to words and discussions; it is peace itself and that is why he will establish his domain, governing the world with an iron scepter to cease all conflicts among men. In the meantime, where is peace in the world? In the lives of those who received it, whether they are black or white, Jewish or Palestinian, born in New Zealand or in Paris, in all those who receive the Shalom of Yeshua.

One of the most interesting passages is the question asked of Yeshua: ***Is it legal to pay taxes to Rome?***

A tricky question, whose answer would mean alignment with the Roman oppressor and invader or an alignment with the rebellious and nationalist zealots of the time. The question was based on the taxes charged by the Roman government, the pagan invader. Behind the apparent ingenuity of the question, a quite complex issue was at stake.

If Yeshua had said, "Only pay the temple," he could have been accused of sedition and handed over to the Romans for crimes against the state.

If he had said, "Pay Rome," he would be considered a traitor to his people and his origins.

In a strategy of magisterial rhetoric, he asked what image was on the coin so that others could answer without him having to actually say "the emperor." Yeshua said:

> ***Well, if the name of Rome is written there and the face of the Roman king is imprinted there, it must be his property, so return to him what belongs to him … and give God what belongs to God.***

Thus, he clearly said that the political disputes of the time were irrelevant compared to issues of the kingdom. He did not come to take up arms, battle it out as a revolutionary and human emancipator, but rather his mission had incomparable nobility, since he came to fight against the *Yetzer Harah* (inclination to do evil) and came to speak about a more important kingdom. However, pride is often confused with vanity.

Yeshua spoke in parables, because he understood people's way of thinking. A parable is a story that helps us understand reality. We can extract the truth from it, since we are capable of understanding. We can only understand life from our own perspective.

Yeshua was a master of the *drash* level of interpretation, one of the four levels of the understanding (*Pardes*) and interpretation of the teachings of God in the teaching of the Torah.

His *midrashim* (comments/sermons) are still referenced, explained, dissected, and discussed today. One of the most beautiful stories probably occurred contextualized within *Yom Kippur*.

Two men went to temple to pray. One of them was a proud and just man in his own eyes, and the other was a tax collector known for his dishonesty. The proud man said the following prayer:

> ***Thank God that I am not a sinner like all the others, especially like that dishonest tax collector over there in the corner. I have never cheated anyone or committed adultery. I fast twice a week; I give to the temple one-tenth of all I earn.***

However, the tax collector stayed in the corner of the temple and did not even dare raise his eyes while he prayed in deep regret:

> ***God, please have mercy on me, a sinner that is worth nothing.***

The tax collector was a man considered to be a traitor, the scum of society, despised and rejected. He represented a link with the Roman invader, since his activity financed the structure and maintenance of Rome's military apparatus. But Yeshua said:

> ***I tell you that the tax collector who recognized the need for God's mercy returned to his home pardoned, since he who exalts himself shall be humiliated, but he who humiliates himself shall be exalted.***

Yeshua criticizes excessive self love, because he believed that people who accept dependence on God must be humble. God does not want us in the gutter, but rather he wants us emptied of our ego. What Yeshua called excessive self love, psychology calls narcissism, which happens when one person has a grandiose vision of him or herself. We have a need to underestimate those who we do not understand. In one way or another, we are "Narcissuses."

A spiritual principle, whose arrogance leads us to believe that we are superior to others, originates from the fear of being inferior.

The word narcissistic refers to someone who is too concerned with him or herself, considers him or herself superior to everyone else, including friends and family. The word narcissist comes from Narcissus, the character of Greek mythology.

Echoes of Pride

> *Narcissus was a very handsome man. Many women wanted to date him, but he was very vain and proud, rejecting all of them. One of the rejected ones was a girl named Echo. Echo became depressed and locked herself in her room without eating or drinking. She was slowly consumed with pain, until she disappeared. Only her voice was heard between the walls of the room. That is where the word "echo" came from. Nemesis, the goddess of revenge, heard Echo's prayers and decided to punish Narcissus so that he would suffer just as she did.*

One day, Narcissus went to the river to drink water. When he crouched down, he saw his own face reflected in the water. Nemesis used her powers so that Narcissus fell desperately in love with his own image. Narcissus could not stop looking at himself. He wanted to touch his image and embrace it, but he could not, since it disappeared when he touched the water. It also was not clearly reflected, since the waves of the river were turbid. He could not kiss himself, since the image disappeared. Therefore, one day while admiring himself, he jumped into the river and drowned.

***

What is the important image for us? The image reflected in the water or the image and resemblance of God? What is the right step to take? Do we keep focused on our ego or on the instruction from God?

Vanity is not exclusively feminine. The metrosexuals of today are the "Narcissuses" of yesterday. Metrosexual is a modern term that refers to a heterosexual urban man who is excessively concerned with his appearance and who spends a great deal of his time and money on his vanity: cosmetics, accessories, and designer label clothes. Within certain limits, vanity means having self-esteem, which is positive and healthy. Up to a certain point it is something quite natural, it is part of our sexuality, since our species, the homo-stupidus, is extremely vain and needs to impress the opposite sex. Therefore, vanity has a social function; it is present both in our needs as well as our professional, romantic, and social relationships.

However, vanity will always be a mantle. We cover ourselves with vanity. It is the spray paint with which we choose to present ourselves, with ingredients of different colors, trends, and tastes. It is a fantasy that is not only associated with a concept of beauty, but with other concepts, still more lethal and destructive. There are vanities that go much further than moisturizing cream, facial powder, or several waxing sessions.

There is the vanity of the ostentatious display of wealth. In this case, people cover themselves with a mantle that is always much bigger than its real size. They seek to use designer label clothing; clothes that are not designer label but pretend to be, they seek to eat at good restaurants and travel to sophisticated places.

There is the vanity of social status, where modern viscounts, marquises, and barons give way to the new elite that emerges through positions, titles, and extensive resumes. They are the "Honorable Sirs," something quite impressive. Even when the most humble worker wants to be polite when dealing with this new nobility, he will call them by the nickname "Doctor"!

There is also religious vanity. When the mantle color called vanity ends in the wealth section and also in the status section, the modern Narcissus looks for the religion spray in the store. They boast about being the representatives of God on Earth or having powers to control nature through the supernatural. Like all uncontrolled vanity, this enslaves us and leads us to adopt senseless attitudes, which obfuscate reason and eliminate discernment.

Vanity is not minimalist; it is abusively creative!

A person who is ill with vanity tends to believe that he or she deserves the special attention of friends, relatives, and colleagues. His or her perception of the world is as if his or her life were a journey illuminated by the brightness of spotlights and running along a red carpet. The vain individual treats others who can reduce the light of this journey with disdain.

However the word of God teaches us to use the key that benefits us and produces a realignment of our priorities. The cure for vanity is found in the repositioning of our priorities. This is the secret:

> ***Let not the wise man boast of his wisdom, or the strong man boast of his strength, or the rich man boast of his riches, but let him who boasts boast about this: that he understands and knows me that I am the LORD, who exercises kindness, justice, and righteousness on earth, for in these I delight.***

CHAPTER 10

Cow Project

Moses was a humble, responsible, and respected leader. However, even though highly accredited, even though he asked, pled, and insisted with God, he did not enter the Promised Land. God did not answer his prayer. Moses had the morale and CV (curriculum vitae) to make this request.

We also call out, but even without Moses' status. Surprisingly, God allows us to get farther that even Moses himself. Most times, we do not realize that the vision of the Promised Land already exists. It is clearer than a picture on the wall is easier to see than a map spread out on top of a table. If we do not take advantage of it, it is not because access was denied, but because we are still not sufficiently prepared for this journey.

Where is the Promised Land? Even with the correct coordinates, with the latitude and longitude indicated by a GPS, borders are always abstractions. They are dynamic and mutable, and the markings of maps are never visible on the floor.

Chaim Weizmann the first president of the State of Israel said:

I want a state, even if it's the size of a tablecloth.

Through this declaration, he affirms that size and limits do not matter. What is relevant is the sovereignty and exclusive right of authority over a geographic area.

Its limits are not physical; its borders are not delimited. We must live sovereign and owners of our own noses, not worrying about the size of our Promised Land. Yes, we have the "gift" of wasting life, because we focus so much on the future that we end up neglecting the present. The present cannot be pushed into the background.

We waste life because we prefer to imagine the flavor rather than try its taste right then and there. We want the joy promised in the word of God as something future, distant, playful, but we refuse to eat a slice of this milk and honey cake now, as if we were a spoiled, stubborn child. The flavor of manna was described as being like honey cakes. Obviously, God would not describe the Promised Land as a dish served with two bananas sliced through the middle, topped with three scoops of ice cream, chocolate caramel and strawberry syrup, chopped nuts, lots of whipped cream, and cherries on top. Nobody would understand.

However, what kind of land is this Promised Land? In the Torah, it is described as: "a land of milk and honey." A land of milk and honey, in a desert region, can be considered a precious promise by God.

Man's internal state is dissatisfaction. We are alive, we can think, talk, walk, breath, see, and hear, however, we only realize how phenomenal and miraculous it is to be alive and healthy when we lose something that before was guaranteed. Even when we are healthy, we sometimes think ourselves the most miserable creatures on earth because we are unable to acquire a particular consumer good.

It is easy to see the issue of dissatisfaction by taking children as an example. It is like a parent who wants to make his child happy and so he takes his son to a modern amusement park full of attractions, one that is famous and always full. The boy goes on several different rides, buys lots of souvenirs, goes on countless rollercoasters, eats an insane amount of chocolate, hamburgers and ice cream, and suddenly, before going to sleep, begins crying uncontrollably because he was not allowed to eat a cookie.

Ah, these children! Are we really that different?

Sometimes, a mansion is our promised land. When we buy it, we become euphoric. Then, the initial excitement is over and we observe that our car does not go with the new garage and we become unsatisfied and sad. We are eternally hunting for what we do not have and we always want more. We are eternally frustrated, we are people who sacrifice happiness, because for us happiness is pleasure, and pleasure is not found in the simple things. We always want new emotions and we get excited about the possibility of having some fun. However, the fun and emotion succumb to our daily reality. Ninety-five percent of our time is used to administer our daily routine. Working, cleaning, buying the basics, eating, paying billings, filling up the tank, sweeping, and managing our problems and our relatives' problems. It is for real life that we have to be prepared. We must take pleasure in daily routines, in day-to-day existence. We must be reeducated to take pleasure in simple things. Simple like a cup of coffee, a good meal, a beautiful song, a good book, or time spent with friends.

It is necessary to learn to take pleasure in our work, in our study, in arriving and leaving our home and even in traffic.

The size of the tablecloth cannot influence our appetite or our satisfaction. Life is not a big party with major events seven days per week.

Some people get discouraged very quickly. They change marriages, because one got boring; they change schools, because the first one got boring, they change jobs because this one got boring; they change religious congregations, because the thrill is gone there too.

Emotion is life's dessert. It is possible to be happy without excitement and strong emotions. It is possible to be happy without fireworks or pompous eveningwear. It is possible to be happy with the simple things in life.

A life headed towards the Promised Land is a life of resignation. The path to God means sacrificing many things and making choices.

Giving up something that is expensive to us has always been hard. Giving up something that, in our understanding, is so good, makes us feel so good, knowing that this will never again be ours is even more difficult. Therefore, giving up something that is actually our own life is nearly impossible.

One day God himself approached a friend and asked him for something: his son, Isaac. A request that is too hard to understand. Would we understand?

God promised his friend Abraham that he would populate the earth with his offspring, that they would be more numerous than the stars in the sky. This promise is now a note of exchange. The first star in the constellation of Sarah, Abraham's wife, was requested as sacrifice. He who Abraham had so anxiously awaited, his most precious good, was to be killed.

It is even dramatic if we think about the years of joy Abraham had while seeing Isaac grow—taking his first steps, then playing, running, and jumping, becoming an even better companion and friend, the boy who called him daddy and laughed with him.

Abraham was happy. He was young, since he was an old man whose soul had been rejuvenated by the arrival of a son. But now his friend tells him:

Give me your son!

If God had given Abraham the so awaited Isaac in the first place, I dare say that he would not have been capable of sacrificing him. Many years of battles, ordeals, doubts, and spiritual experiences were required for Abraham to be able to grow and see promises fulfilled.

The Abraham who received God's promise is not the same one who climbed the mountain to sacrifice his son. The new Abraham is different than the old one. The Abraham of Mount Moriah was a tested, improved, and ready man. The love between parents and children is not established by interest, but occurs because children are the essence of parents. Let us change scenarios. Let us go to *Hamakom* (the place). The geographic reference changes, but the meaning of the events is similar. Mount Moriah changes names and becomes Golgotha, where another lamb is sacrificed. Is that the end of sacrifices?

If we go back even farther in time, the English name for the book of *Vayikra* (Leviticus) originates from the word Levi. Levi's tribe was responsible for fulfilling the orders of the sacrificial system down to the last detail.

God had to give the initial kickoff. He needed to start the *Tikkun Olam*, the restoration of humanity, and allow the possibility of reconciliation. That is why he needed a people. Leviticus narrates the events when he began the process of propagating his purposes. Instead of using a strong people, who buried their leaders in giant tombs in the format of pyramids at the edge of the Nile River, he chose a more difficult path.

Instead of using a cultured people like the Greeks, a people who produced philosophers and mathematicians, whose intelligence generated the basis for Western philosophical thinking, he chose a more difficult path.

Instead of using a people from the Far East who were numerous and large, whose wall is the only human construction visible in satellite photos, he chose a more difficult path and decided to produce offspring through the grandson of Abraham. However, Abraham was very elderly and did not have children when God made a promise, affirming to him:

> ***Look into the heavens and see the countless stars that exist there: your descendents will be numerous.***

And Abraham believed, believed in the truth, and that is why he is considered the father of faith. God said that of his offspring, someone would be born who would bless all the peoples of the earth. That is why he establishes the *Brit Milah*, the pact of circumcision. The word "alliance" in Hebrew is *Brit*, which, within the Jewish context, is related to the word blood—"alliance of blood." An alliance is an agreement, a contract, a testament. Receiving the instruction from God means agreeing on an alliance. Certainly, it would have been more convenient and practical if Abraham's pact were based on the extraction of just a few drops of blood from the point of the nose or ear lobe. However, circumcision occurs precisely at the site where the seed leaves. Thus, there is a very clear meaning, since it is from where the seed would leave that would indicate he who would bless all the nations of earth.

The faith that pleases God is the faith of certainty. It is not a flaccid, inconsistent faith that is full of doubt. The faith that pleases God removes obstacles; it moves mountains. The patriarchs had this faith. Moses had this faith. Joshua had this faith. David had this faith and we can all have this faith.

Those who have faith are committed: they are indissoluble, inseparable. There is no room for doubt when certainty is there. There is no excuse for a lack of commitment when there is faith.

God ordered Isaac's sacrifice, testing Abraham. It initially seems very strange, unjust and bizarre, but God, who always worked justly through just means, wants to reveal something; he wants to indicate something that will happen in the future. Isaac does not die, and he produces Jacob.

Jacob is a man in search of his identity, a normal man like us, full of virtues and defects, but a man transformed by faith and obedience. Jacob had a life full of numerous battles and in a certain way, we can see ourselves in him. He did not live in a glass bell gar or a plastic bubble acclimatized with filtered air. Jacob deconstructed his self-sufficiency and faced life head-on.

There are circumstances in our lives from which we want to flee. The first option is the easiest, and the temptation is to give up. Abandoning everything, we ignore the problems; by backing out, everything is resolved. This is the ostrich's tactic: it does not want to see and assume its responsibilities.

Appearances, however, are misleading. The ostrich has interesting behavior: by burying its head in the sand, it creates a camouflage that resembles from afar a small mound or bush, which would be impossible with its neck up. However, if the predator gets closer, the ostrich takes off running at a fast speed. Jacob acted just like an ostrich: either he would hide or he would run. This process only stopped when God decided to give him shock treatment. The shocking message, revealed through a dream, was basically the following: "It is no use fleeing, you have to believe in me to resolve your problems."

The dream changed Jacob's life. What worked for Jacob, works for us. When we stop trying to escape the problem, we can dream and see that which was hidden. This means bringing into existence that which did not exist.

Those who do not dream do not accomplish; they do not reach an objective. To dream is to begin to believe in that which you did not create. The dream is the beginning of it all. It means living again, having motivation again. It means reestablishing life.

What Jacob was experiencing was an unharnessed escape; it was just fear. God showed Jacob what he had not seen: a heavenly staircase.

The words of God were not exactly these, but they would certainly sound something like:

> ***I am God of Abraham, Isaac, and Jacob. I am the God of alliance, God of promise. God of the word. What I said to Isaac, I now say to you, Jacob: In you all the nations will be blessed. I have not forgotten.***

It does not matter what situation we are experiencing. What matters is that we are connected to God through a stairway of faith. Thus, Psalm 91 emerges, since we will have angels at our service. This staircase could never be an escalator. There is no effort involved there. There is no spiritual ascension. You just stand there. And without effort and movement, nothing happens. In life, nothing is free; everything has a price. The staircase must be climbed. When we go up one step, the only certainty we have is that remaining there motionless will not take us anywhere. The movement must continue. On the other hand, the peak of our spiritual journey is not a place to be reached in a single leap.

When God wanted to talk to Abraham's grandson as an individual, he called him Yaakov, but when he wanted to talk to Jacob as if this represented a legal entity, he called him Israel. God's vision has a corporate focus. In other words, regardless of how much individuality characterizes man, we need to have collective concerns. The whole molds the part. Accordingly, the part is always a byproduct of the whole. Pillars of individuality are weakened when we gradually assimilate the instruction from God.

Jacob was responsible for his descendants. This was not an individual commitment, but rather a collective one. Through Jacob's example, we learn that our life cannot revolve around our own bellybutton.

The Jacob "corporation," also known as Israel, had 12 children, who gave rise to the 12 tribes. Levi, one of those tribes, had the exclusive priest function. Within the Levi tribe one family stood part: the Cohanim (priests). They were responsible for preserving and maintaining the basics of the relationship between man and God. This is the central topic of all instruction from God—the sacrificial system.

***

Judaism, in its essence, is liturgical and sacrificial. Liturgical, because it is detailed, full of minute observances and obeys the order of services at the temple, the *Beit Hamikdash*. It is sacrificial since it is founded on man's relationship with God and vice-versa.

The Hebrew word for sacrifice, *korban*, comes from the same root as the word *karov*—to get closer to. A *korban* is a means through which we can get closer to God. It is normal to have doubts about this mechanism. After all, what is the mechanism of sacrifice?

When someone makes us upset, our first reaction is to become furious, and distance ourselves from this person. In the same way, when we sin, we distance ourselves from God and this distance negatively affects our relationship with him. The invitation for approaching him again begins with repentance. Sacrifices provided a means for repairing this damaged relationship; they served as a mechanism of reconciliation.

The sacrifice of an animal is a live representation of what transgressors really deserve for violating God's order, with the animal serving as a substitute for the punishment of the offender. When a person saw the korban on the altar, he was supposed to see himself in the animal's place, a thought that was meant to awaken feelings of *Teshuvah* (repentance, return, reconciliation).

It functioned as a *Teshuvah*, if there really was repentance, recognition of error, perception of justice and reconciliation.

It was a substitute, a korban that God gave to Abraham in Isaac's place. The understanding of this mechanism does not have anything intuitive about it. It is necessary to think and reflect extensively about this question. And thinking leads us to the truth …

Let us speak of the truth. Apparently dissonant truths have many more elements in common than we think. What unites the fans of a soccer team, or skinheads, the members of the Board of Directors of a major multinational, and the members of an ecological Non-Governmental Organization (NGO)? Could there be something in common between such different people? Is it possible to identify a common denominator? As incredible as it seems, it is possible. They all have a philosophy. In other words: they all have their own truth. They all believe in their truth and they all fight for their truth, which determines the lifestyle that they lead.

The truth of the skinhead is the truth of power, and he exercises power through racism. This is the ideology of power in which the skinhead believes and which is full of concepts of supremacy. His energy is hatred. He wants to annihilate the object of hatred and multiply power. The executive of a major multinational company wants power and leadership for his company. The grandeur of his company multiplies with the elimination of the competition. The executive exercises power with marketing, research and investment techniques. His energy is financial interest.

An "organized" group of soccer fans identifies with their team, as if each victory of the team were a personal victory. The joy of the fans is the defeat of the rival, and its energy is the suffering imposed on the other team. The power and dominion of the fans are expressed by demonstrating their love for their team. The fans' mission is to verbally and physically defend the honor of the soccer team, which can lead them to become involved in violent acts, which certain fans consider to be heroic. The importance of NGOs these days is unquestionable. Their power comes from the ease of recruiting donations and volunteers. Their efficiency is based on the communication and propagation of their ideas. The major challenge faced by NGOs is revealing themselves to society and convincing it of their cause, bringing power and prestige. Their energy is the sensation of justice.

But does an absolute truth exist?

First, it is necessary to clearly perceive that the entire process of understanding will always be unequal, and our truths are always relative. However, this cannot serve as an excuse for us not to think.

The truth—we must reconstruct the truth and deconstruct the misleading processes that have surrounded us for centuries.

Some apparent truths are actually false, such as: We do not need intermediaries.

I do not need the rabbi or the guru or the pastor or the shaman or the medicine man or, the mashiach. I guarantee my place with God; I have credit in his bank, I sign the check and he pays.

These concepts are not declared in the instruction from God. These truths diverge from the experiences of the patriarchs Abraham, Isaac, and Jacob. The rabbi is not a leader, a teacher in the Jewish community today. However, in the past, the attribution of the *Cohanim* (priests) was to exercise mediation. The story of Abraham's intercession for Sodom, which appears in Genesis, is interesting, but the most important example is precisely when Moses interceded for Israel. On this day Moses was the attorney who masterfully defended the absolution of a people and certainly gave one of the best examples of an attorney that has ever been seen. This genial intervention led to *Yom Kippur*, the day of forgiveness, the most sacred day in the Jewish calendar. The episode showed that the people were unsatisfied and depressed by loneliness (or by Moses' absence), and that is why they initiated the *Cow Project.*

The *Cow Project* began with a voluntary offering, the occasion on which Aaron asked the people to bring in their jewels for casting.

This project was a copy of the Mishkan project (the mobile tabernacle), albeit distorted, since both tend to show a visible image of God living among his people. In this case, a cow cast in pure gold represents the climax of human self-sufficiency, probably at its highest level.

The *Cow Project* is human passion, desire and boldness defeating the Creator. The man who was always in search of God, who always "hunted" God, finally caught him. All of the attempts at this persecution of the divine throughout history have ended in religion. Religion is this: the *Cow Project.* After all, the wise man, the "homo-sapiens," always will prefer a cow.

Leaving the cow and returning to man, the path to communication with God had the same direction, but with opposite meanings. Priests were the intermediaries of man's connection with God, while prophets did the opposite—they represented God's communication with man.

It is a mistake to believe that the sacrificial system was a huge slaughterhouse, a refrigerated warehouse, a mechanical and systematic production line that produced mounds of animal carcasses to serve the whims of a backward and primitive society.

The process had a clear premise and efficient logic. When an individual ritualistically offered a sacrifice under the supervision of a priest, the process of immolation of the korban over the altar was something beneficial, since who should have died for the transgressions was the very individual offering the sacrifice. However, now there was a substitute.

The instruction from God said that without the shedding of blood there would be no remission of sins. And why blood? Life is found in blood. Blood is life or death. The only remedy for death is life, and curiously, the only remedy for life is death. If you repent, recognize your error, realize the notion of justice and credit and believe in the power of reconciliation, then blood is life. If the issue of blood does not make any sense and does not serve to obtain forgiveness, then blood is death.

In Egypt, it was the blood on the doorposts of the children of Israel that freed them from death. The instruction from God does not condition the preservation of life on kindness, moral improvement, or the intensification of prayers but rather exclusively on the presence of blood on the doors. The mezuzah, a religious symbol attached to the sides of the doors of observant Jews' homes, is a symbol in reminder of this blood.

With the end of Temple, the sacrifices stopped. Many thought and continue to think the same thing, that human kindness, purified morale and ceaseless prayers are the same as restoring the temple. However, the greatest best seller of all times, the publication that transmits the instruction from God, the Bible, does not teach this.

According to this line of reasoning, according to the teaching from God, the entire sacrificial system typifies Yeshua's death. Blood does not lose its importance; it does not lose its function. Once again: blood is life. This was and still is the exit, a definitive and single sacrifice. This sacrifice took place approximately 2,000 years ago, but it is still continually updated and fully exercised if to you blood is life. After all, it is all of us who should die for our countless errors.

Arthur Schopenhauer (1788-1860), a German philosopher, said:

> ***All truth goes through three phases: during the first phase, it is ridiculed; during the second, it is violently vexed; and during the third, it is accepted as proof itself.***

Legitimacy is a very interesting issue. What is legitimate today was probably illegitimate in the past. Legitimate is an equation that involves interests. Interest is associated with power. Accordingly, what is legitimate is that which interests power.

We need to reconstruct the truth and deconstruct deceptive processes that have surrounded us for centuries. After all, as a famous rabbi once said:

> ***Know the truth and the truth will set you free.***

In my quest for truth, one day I decided to pay attention to something else the same rabbi said:

> ***I am the way and the truth and the life. Nobody comes to the Father except through me.***

The path to this truth is narrow; there are no shortcuts or alternative routes. In Hebrew, the word truth is *EMET*, and is written with the words Aleph, Mem, and Tav, which are respectively the first, the middle, and the last letter of the Hebrew alphabet. In Greek, the initial and final letters of the alphabet are the well known Alfa and Omega. *EMET* is everything that has a beginning, middle, and end. A truth without beginning, middle, or end is not consistent.

This rabbi was a man who did not deny his origins, who did not invent a new religion, who did not break from the eternal alliance of Sinai, who orthodoxically fulfilled all the *mitzvoth* (commandments), and who with authority warned and admonished others about the consequences of the failure to comply with these. This rabbi was a man who was born a Jew, who lived a Jew and who, upon the occasion of his death, had the following written on his epitaph: *Melech Hayehudim!* This means: "The King of the Jews."

This rabbi was a man who said he was: the truth, the way, the life. This truth, however, is not a dogma. This truth cured the blind and the paralyzed, it brought back the dead, and primarily, this truth explained the instruction from God like nobody ever had before.

CHAPTER 11

WONDERLAND OR PROMISE LAND?

We are not only rational beings; we are also emotional ones. Humans have a strong tendency to consider emotion a weakness. We were raised to control our emotions and learn to deal with them. However, could it be that we have the capacity and need to control them? Or should we become increasingly more emotional beings?

Emotions are not a seven-headed beast like it is thought, nor are they something inconstant. Without feelings, we would be beings deprived of grace, charm, life, and flavor. No human being has total control over or can fully dominate their emotions. The most mathematical and rational scientist cannot do this, the great international chess masters cannot, and not even the coldest and most calculated assassin can.

In the 1970s sci-fi television series *Star Trek*, there is a curious fellow with pointy ears named Mr. Spock, who was first mate and science officer on the USS Enterprise. He personified cold and rational intelligence, free from any emotion. He came from the planet Vulcan, a member planet of the Stellar Federation that was allied with planet Earth, which, in the distant past, had nearly been destroyed by conflicts and wars thought to be sparked by emotions. Accordingly, the population made it a mission to eliminate emotions.

Fiction and reality, however, do not always go hand-in-hand. Emotion is the fuel of our lives. Life without it is no life at all. Everybody wants to assume total control over their lives.

We were raised to believe that the essence of control is to trust in ourselves, but the truth is that we do not control anything.

It is not only the emotions that we want to control. Our thirst for control is great, since we need this mechanism to feel powerful.

We are essentially controlling beings. So controlling that nobody in their home fights to use the blender, the toaster or the juicer, but they all fight over the TV remote control. Many daily problems arise because the tendency to be in control destroys us; the paths we designate bring us no solution. We change the channel; we adjust the programming, but we do not always get it right. Another example of a television program is reality shows. Theoretically, these are soap operas without scripts, where the viewers suppose that there is no control over participants and that the people who participate in these type of programs act in accordance with their own consciences. They do not represent characters; they are real, made of flesh and blood, but there is a control mechanism that molds and controls their moves. The participants are human guinea pigs in laboratories, where cameras monitor them 24 hours per day.

This concept was initially developed by George Orwell, a British author who wrote a novel called *1984*. In this book, he describes a fictitious society, where everyone is under the constant surveillance of the authorities. All members of this society were constantly bombarded by the government's propaganda slogan: "Big Brother is watching you."

In the current reality shows participants are concerned about the opinion of others. Even a simple trip to the bathroom is an event watched by millions of television viewers. Their freedom collides with the social control that we exercise over their consciences and with the mechanisms of interaction that the program allows us to have.

After all, we want to have control over everything. We were raised to believe that the essence of control means trusting in ourselves.

However, we are not free, nor are we participants in a reality show, much less in relation to our own lives, since we have no control over the events that will come next. The truth is that we do not control anything. Ideology, which has permeated our lives and which makes us believe that we are in control, is yet another bluff. Control is an emotional bluff. And, like every bluff, we have to eliminate it from our lives.

Life obeys certain logic: the instruction from God guides us. We cannot be compulsive gamblers and imagine that our life is governed by chance; like a game of Russian roulette.

Death is not the only, but most certainly the greatest, proof that human self-sufficiency collides with the lack of control. Life without death is not life. There is no way to speak about life without talking about death. It is an essentially dialectic question. We can only understand life through death. It is the only certainty that we have in life. The rest is gain or loss, accomplishments or frustrations.

If there is one experience that throughout history and around the world places the entire human race in the same boat, it is death. Death is extremely democratic: rich, poor, ugly, beautiful—everyone dies. Death is something that we all must face, since no exercise or diet, no meditation technique or amount of money in the world can prevent it from coming.

This is the great truth that makes us all equal. We have no control over it. This can be seen in everything that surrounds us while we try so hard to stop the aging process. We wait eagerly for that next pill, surgery, or genetic discovery that may be the key to prolonging our lives a bit further.

The decay and wear of the human machine is inevitable, but at the same time is part of the preparatory process for afterlife.

Spiritual inclusion in a world beyond our own is linked to the behavior and lifestyle whose main expression is transforming faith. Words are external signs that may or may not reflect an internal transformation. It is no use exhaustively repeating passages from the instruction from God as if they were mantras when there is no resonance between the faith and discourse. The mouth must transmit something that truly planted root into the heart.

Communication is essential; it is a powerful key to transformation. Good communication is a verbalized conviction that will generate transformation. It is not only through words that communication is established. There are ingredients in communication that are much more powerful than verbalization—ingredients that extend from our tone of voice to our posture towards the person with whom we are talking.

Communicating with the Creator requires special care, since the responsibility of having God as a dialogist is the greatest responsibility that we can have in any attempt at communication.

Praying is the channel of communication with God. It is an experience that leads us to a path of intimacy with the truth. It involves an attitude of continuously searching for the power and knowledge that come from God. Praying places us in contact with a God who is sensitive to his children's needs. And it must be a relationship of sincere surrender.

This mechanism is the point of contact with the Creator. It is an attitude of the mind that seeks efficient communication; the solution that transforms reality, that brings positive results, since God interacts with us like a father does with his children. It is the solution used by those who know where control comes from.

Our authority is linked to our capacity to be sincere. Communication is vital. And in the process of communication, it is much more important to have the attention and understanding of the person listening than the facility of the person talking to express themselves.

If communication is vital, it is important to understand that God's language is not an intuitive language. God will never be a "trouble shooter," an occasional problem solver.

This "trouble shooter" God can only be a pre-Babylon pagan divinity, a slave to human needs and stupidity. Instead of assimilating the instruction that comes from God, man prefers to transform God into a winning lottery ticket. We use God and we remember him like we do with the yellow pages when we need to call a plumber for a leaky pipe, or an electrician when the circuit breaker burns out.

It is man creating God in his image and resemblance, inverting the roles and acting just like a child, creating God as if he were a piece of modeling clay. This God is the fruit of the idolatry that we have for our ego.

> **God is lentils!** Yes, for Esau, God is lentils.
> **God is corrupt!** Yes, the God created by the corrupt man is corrupt.
> **God is violence!** Yes, for a murderer, the God that he creates is violent.
> **God is hate!** Yes, for those who spread fear, the God they create is hate.

All of these Gods are the fruits of the man's desire to control the gods of the Self-Sufficiency Olympus.

There is no space for spasms of commitment, nor occasional moments to remember an alliance.

If God simply wanted to make his existence known to all people on the planet, he would simply call a press conference worldwide to present himself, becoming visible and audible. However, God's direct presence would inevitably reduce our free will, replacing faith with vision. What the eyes see, in this case, is blindness, but the vision of faith is perfect.

Faith is the certainty of things
that still do not exist and which are not seen.

Faith during times of plenty is a mere verification, at the most an expression of thanks. It is not put to the test and does not require any effort. Faith is effectively proven during difficult and testing times. Try saving on your agenda time for the most important task that you will have every day of your life: try interacting with God. Nothing can be more crucial during your existence; and nothing deserves more importance or care. What afflicts you today? Who does not have concerns that cause pain, disappointments, and hurt?

If these concerns cause you suffering, then communicate. Talk about your anxieties and needs. Every day, we have an excellent opportunity to establish a connection with God, and this is important considering that the control is not in our hands.

In short, what we need to be happy, both now as well as after physical death, is to cultivate our *Tikkun Haadam* (reform of man).

All reform is hard work; it is messy and inconvenient, but necessary. We always want to be in control of everything. Have you ever stopped to think about the number of things you put off every day and how many things you never complete, never finish, or never do? Human beings have a lousy habit of putting off those things they think are hard to do.

We always think that we can leave them for later; that we will have a second chance, that the world will wait for our awakening. Putting things off is a coward's attitude. We have to fight off this tendency to be expectant and not participants in the decisions that affect our lives. It is as if the Creator of the universe is saying to us now:

> ***Welcome to your life. Invite me, call me in, and give me control; let us work together.***

The paradox of this relationship is that, in order to be agents of our own story, to confront situations—deal the cards, define the paths—we must transfer control.

Do not avoid this responsibility. Do not give up on the transformation. Do not give up the chance to bury uncertainties and fears that represent an old nature.

You do not have control over everything, but this is wonderful. Challenge unfavorable circumstances, since you are certainly not adrift in a boat.

The word of God categorically affirms that nothing happens on Earth without God's permission. He is sovereign over all things:

> ***Who can speak and make things happen if God had not so decreed? I say: My purpose will stay standing, and I will do everything that pleases me. God's plans remain forever; the purpose of his heart, for all generations.***

***

All ideas developed until the present about control and death aim to implode the pillars of human self-sufficiency. Death appears to be a final border, but the good news is that it is also just a stage involved in constructing man's relationship with God. What seems to some to be an insurmountable wall is the maturity process of the *Tikkun Haadam*.

Our soul is immortal. If we are able to interiorize the idea that the process of immortality is something available, something real in our lives, then death no longer has a place in our world. Eternal life is expensive because it demands effort, sacrifice, and commitment.

In a way it can be said that aging is a process of liberation. The idea of facing this process as a death sentence is limiting, since it eliminates the possibility of being able to live for other values and other interests. Gradual aging is an experience that must be faced with serenity and acceptance, since physical strength is not crucial for achieving happiness.

If a 16-year-old lies down in his bed for a year without doing anything productive, at the end of the year he will be 17 years old. If a 77-year-old man lies in his bed for a year without doing anything productive, he will be 76 at the end of the year. Both become equal, get old, but they do not seek to improve themselves. The idea of growing is more closely linked to the capacity for creation and production than to the numbers on a clock. The experienced person will often say that he or she learned more due to what he or she did not do than due to what he or she produced and did. One thing is certain: idleness and laziness are not the best alternatives for growth. Mature thinking is balanced. In many societies, the elderly represent the wise and can predict situations due to their experience. We physically come to have limits, but the capacity for intellectual rejuvenation is not affected. Sadness is not linked to old age, but rather to the spiritual state of the individual.

The stereotype of the elderly person as a grouch is as false as any other stereotype and is normally prejudiced.

A grouchy teenager always has the excuse that the process of puberty brings about hormonal changes that would justify rude behavior and constant complaining. A grouchy adult who fights for survival to sustain his or her family in an environment marked by tough professional competition always uses this excuse to justify his or her bad mood. However, an elderly person without such excuses ends up being unjustly labeled as a grouch.

A grouchy teenager becomes a grouchy adult, who then becomes a grouchy old person. Grumpiness has internal and not chronological origins.

Death scares young people as much as it does adults and the elderly. There is no one who has never felt the impact of death. After the death of a friend or loved one, we feel emptiness in our heart; a feeling of loneliness that takes over and which makes us aware of the finiteness of life.

There is no real transformation in life without the destruction of old certainties. We must oxygenate our minds. It is an alignment with new principles. When we take the car out to align our tires, the idea is to service the car "in line," without it "pulling" to one side. Having a renewed mind means investing your precious time thinking without allowing your thoughts to wander off course and follow the paths of lies and evil.

It is time to hear the wake-up call. Start right now with the transformations you would like to happen, carefully choosing your thoughts. The result will be a renewed mind, one capable of making major changes. Be the leader of yourself. Efficient leaders concentrate their thoughts on noble, authentic, virtuous, and praiseworthy things. The result is that they provoke a powerful and irresistible influence over those around them.

The teaching from God says that there is always a right time, a time to live, and a time to die, a time to plant and a time to reap what was planted, a time to cry and a time to laugh.

However, we want to laugh all the time and we do not tolerate moments of happiness interwoven with moments of ordeal. Those who know when to cry laugh harder. Yes, that is right. Those who cry at the right time will know to laugh at the perfect moment.

Life is a gift! Declare this! What we do is always done here and now. Learning to live the "now" gives us the perception that a single instance is infinite. Today is the priority.

The present is the moment to decide the path to be followed. The issue of the path to take comes to light again in the story of *Alice in Wonderland.*

Alice meets another character: The Cheshire Cat.

> ***Smiling Cat, please do tell me, what path shall I take?*** asked Alice.
>
> ***That depends on where you want to go*** responded the cat.
>
> ***I do not much care where I am going*** responded Alice.
>
> ***Then it does not matter which path you take*** said the cat.

An enormous lesson: If you do not know where you want to go, any path works. We need to know where we are. We need to know where we are going. Therefore, if you want to find the teachings from God, you must identify the path to be followed. And identify it soon, because the cat is laughing at you.

***

If it were possible to enter into a hypothetical time tunnel and take a tour through the past, we would discover that Moses based his discourse on two premises: the first is that the word from God guarantees prosperity; and the second is that there is also the guarantee of good health for all who follow and fully believe in these words. Moses' advice is for us to concentrate on looking through history and realize that we must trust in God. However, we must be careful to not become distracted by our financial prosperity, putting God in second place.

As a compiler of the instruction that comes from God, Moses warns about idolatry. Idolatry from the perspective of a practical theological definition is the act of serving images, praying to them, making promises to saints and gurus, participating in processions, etc. From this perspective, idolatry means ceasing from submitting to the Creator, bowing to icons created by man.

However, the best definition for idolatry is the belief that any other thing beside God has power. From this perspective it is quite clear that we live in a world that is extremely idolatrous, since idolatry is conceptually a much more broad-reaching aspect that simply bowing to clay, ceramic or wooden statues.

Idolatry is synonymous with self-sufficiency.

The Torah teaches us:

It is not because of their justice or righteousness that you will overthrow their lands, but rather because of the evil of these nations that the Lord, your God, will drive them out before your eyes, to fulfill the promise that the Lord made, under oath, to your ancestors, Abraham, Isaac and Jacob.

The Israelis were given the Land of Canaan in fulfillment of God's promise to Abraham's descendents. No meritorious criteria were used to fill places based on grades and classifications. Man's virtue was not used as God's criteria for distributing the deeds of the properties in the Promised Land. Our justice is a very fine and fragile fiber that does not in any way entitle us to plead favors in terms of distributing the good and obtaining happiness. Therefore, our idolatry, a sub-product of our self-sufficiency, must be renounced, removed, and eliminated. There is a lot of talk about a life of renunciation. But what exactly does this mean?

The life of renunciation is the act of returning to God the life that he gave us. It means abandoning control, rights, power, and the steering wheel, everything that you do and say. It means fully surrendering life in his hands, so that he may lead it forward as he wishes.

The path to renunciation begins with God bringing us a sensation of complete fragility. Renunciation is, more than anything, an act of courage. And few are able to practice renunciation. It is easy to become attached. The hard part is becoming unattached.

Renouncing means uttering a rounded and convincing, "No!" Even though it is a simple word, it is extremely hard to say.

"No" is a transforming word, one which opens doors, which causes rupture, which determines non-consensual choices, which is not convenient, which generates power. "No" is much more powerful than yes.

"No" generates change. It has energy. It is strong and powerful, while yes is weak, convenient; it does not have an impact.

Therefore, if you want transformation in your life, become aware of the need to affirm the "no" without guilt, even if this ends up hurting someone.

We have to reject the "yes" and affirm the "no."

The "no" cries out within us, but our mouth says yes because we feel guilty about saying "no."

We must avoid a culture of consensus. We frequently agree with things simply to keep those at our side happy. Unfortunately, this is not always beneficial.

It is important to point out that 90% of the chances and opportunities that appear in our life deserve a "no," while only 10% of the cases deserve a "yes." The "yes" is a final stage in a long filtering process where dozens of "noes" were spoken that opened paths to the inevitable yes. If the "no" filter stays deactivated, when we say yes to the world, we deny the life that God gives us.

The stigma surrounding the word "no" is associated with an unfriendly word because it rejects something.

Neurolinguistics even suggests rewriting certain phrases to prevent being direct, as shown in the example below:

Phrase: *Do not go out without your umbrella.*

Rewritten phrase: *Remember to take your umbrella when you leave.*

"No" is associated with a negative mental image. By suppressing the word, a new image is created that is positive. People really are quite scared of "no." On the other hand, I think it is fantastic! It has a transforming action that surprises our colleagues and we always keep the element of surprise in our favor with it. They are the two letters that really make the difference. Like many words, it does not reach everyone, but we must believe in the power of freedom from conformism, since yes very clearly carries within it this conformism. We must break from the alienation of comfort, destroy the conservatism of the yes, using the power of this apparently simple word, but one that has a profound meaning and produces transformation. To blossom, the truth needs a no. I believe that this act is a process of metamorphosis, and that to enjoy this growth, we need to begin with the no.

Our problems occur mainly due to the fact that we agree to many things at the same time. That is why we fail by not saying no. We have the habit of responding this way to the requests that others make: "Of course I can do it," or "Relax, I'll take care of this," and once again, we use the bluff resource, since we deliberately trick ourselves, we establish no position. We do not transform; we do not free ourselves from the indolence and lack of energy of the yes.

Our response is unreal and impulsive, because deep down we know very well that we do not want to do that which was asked of us, because in our line of priorities and at the boundaries of our limits, we know that we cannot assume other tasks.

Know that saying "no" without guilt is not egoism, but rather a necessary protection.

Global revolution starts with inner revolution. If we are incapable of transforming our "I," we will not be capable of transforming the world around us. Transformation occurs from the inside out. If we want to think globally, if we want to think macro, we must first act within our own micro-universe. We must the purify the "I."

We must look in the microscope and think about the small details that make the difference. One of humanity's great errors is wanting to do the opposite. Think of the microcosm and act in the macrocosmic sense. Superstition is an overwhelming expression of idolatry; it is a silly confidence in ineffective things. It is exaggerated attachment, which at first seems inoffensive, but which is extremely harmful.

The neuralgic point of the issue is based on the fact that a person who is superstitious thinks deep down that he or she will be able to resolve his or her problems using devices and unfounded beliefs. It is the natural result of separation, divorce from God. To the same extent that a man flees from the instruction that comes from God, he leans toward superstition.

Superstition is faith deviated from its natural course, and this is why man resorts to apparently magical objects and formulas in order to reverse his own problems. It is the desire for independence that shifts faith in another direction and whose fuel is the prayers, amulets, crystals, pendulums, pyramids, and uncountable other variants.

Superstition inhibits free judgment; it generates a fatalism that turns us into spectators similar to workers on strike. A silly, useless strike generated by immaturity: the strike against life. It is not a strike for better conditions, but rather one that leads to imprisonment, whose handcuffs are spiritual, since it makes people cross their arms and become completely idle.

The man who seeks God forgets that God knows where we are. And we can have a spiritual experience at any time, since God is not confined to or secluded in temples, churches, or synagogues. He is entirely free of any limitation of space and time. God is not material; he is not sculpted or carved by the human hand and is also not an abstract force, like the philosophers think. If he were an abstraction, he would be the most real one that exists, since he is the start of movement, action, and transformation. The greatest secrets always surprise us with their simplicity. The concept is simple, but the application is complex. God expects a no from us for all that separates us from him. In this way, we flee from the idolatry of self-sufficiency.

We begin to see God's presence in what we do, think, and feel; we discover that spirituality is obtained through continuous, gradual and consistent effort. We become wiser, stronger and we sharpen our perception, discernment and will. "No" is the key to spiritual intelligence. It is the intelligence that we lack allows us to enjoy and savor the wisdom from God. Having a high spiritual IQ allows us to use time in our favor. We cease being our own biggest adversaries and we will finally be destined for success. Consequently, by developing this spiritual IQ, we stop wasting our lives; otherwise, we will inevitably channel our efforts, energy, and will down the drain of unproductiveness.

There is a term in Hebrew called *Am Segulah* (special people). If this expression is given to us from God, it can be concluded that it is not simply a poetic, religious, and abstract expression. It is crucial to know what it really means to be special. What is the true sense of being a special people, and what is it that differentiates us and makes us special? Being special means believing that all the instruction from God allows us to penetrate the borders of the impossible. Being special means that fulfilling promises is related to our capacity to absorb and accept changes. Nothing will change in your life until you change your way of thinking.

There is no way to experience the new if we do not move from where we were. The past cannot obstruct the fulfillment of your future. Being special means being in tune with the things that must be changed in your life. Get attached to promises, not to problems. Being special means wanting to change.

If God insisted that you come into the world, this means that he values you. You are not an accident, the random fruit of probabilities. You are not the work of chance and much less a permissive oversight of God. You are a gift to the world, equipped with a spiritual IQ made in the Creator's image and resemblance. A work of art signed by God. We have his fingerprints on us.

The instruction from God leaves it clear that individuality is a mark of creation:

Before I formed you in the womb, I knew you, and before you left the womb, I sanctified you.

We are not just another product from a gigantic assembly line. We are not assembled like dolls on a moving conveyor belt, where pre-made parts are placed by specialized workers. Mass production is inflexible and makes it hard to change the design of each part created, since it only allows for the production of identical and similar parts. However, the world is brimming with impressive diversity that, in addition to its external characteristics, expresses differences in individuality.

There is something very special. A unique element that makes us unique, incomparable, differentiated, and rare. Look around you. Look to the side, out the window, look towards the street, and look at the crowd that walks randomly in different directions. Although there are a few coincidences between physical aspects, the appearances are clearly different. Everyone is different. There are no repetitions. No one is born the same as any other, not even identical twins. No artist or manufacturer or person, regardless of how creative he or she may be, is able to conceive such diversity and complexity.

We have no competition; we are unique!

If we purchase a book in the bookstore of the same edition or if we buy one online, we basically have the same book—the same content, the same cover, the same author, and the same publisher. However, if we had the opportunity to go to the book signing, we would have something unique in our hands. We would have a unique copy, one that was personal, with a dedication written especially for us. It is entirely one-of-a-kind, and we would not find this in any bookstore, either real or virtual. We would then have something differentiated given to us by the author himself.

This differentiation also reveals itself in our lives. There are millions of talented, intelligent, pro-active and hard-working people in the world. However, what makes us special is God's signature on our lives. We are a work of art. We were created in his image for a unique purpose. This unique purpose eliminates all competition. We are special! If we are special, we must act like special people. Not because of what we do, but because of what we are: carefully carved and sculpted to express this difference. What is important is not looking for a differential in appearance or form, but rather what really places us in a distinguished position is identifying the purpose and believing firmly in the autograph we carry in our lives and which guarantees us success.

We must be very careful with the travel details and less worried about arriving at the destination, because it is the journey itself that teaches us and not the destination. The destination is simply a consequence of the path taken. If winning in life is not a constant in your day-to-day, then you have already lost.

Winning in life means crossing a sea of tears and not drowning in them. It means having the courage to fight the tide and the wave that appears to knock you over.

Winning is mainly about not doubting the favor that comes from God, since it means recognizing that all perseverance and courage that we need results from God's action in our lives. He multiplies the force of those who consider themselves weak.

Everything we do can be represented by seeds: words, thoughts, and attitudes. Every day is another challenge. You must simply believe in the one that is your refuge and strength.

Complicity with the truth creates commitment—commitment to knowledge, a commitment to instruction, a commitment to God's will.

OTHER RELATED RESOURCES

Available at Messianic Jewish Resources Int'l. • www.messianicjewish.net
1-800-410-7367
(Prices subject to change.)

Coming Soon!

Complete Jewish Study Bible - New Testament

- The New Testament portion of the Complete Jewish Bible, adapted for the American audience.
- Introductions and articles by well known Messianic Jewish theologians including Dr. David Friedman, Dr. John Fischer, Dr. Jeffrey Seif, Dr. Dan Juster, Rabbi Russ Resnik, and more.
-Hebrew Idioms found in the New Testament explained by Israeli Messianic Jewish scholar, Dr. David Friedman.

Complete Jewish Bible: *A New English Version*

—Dr. David H. Stern

Presenting the Word of God as a unified Jewish book, the *Complete Jewish Bible* is a new version for Jews and non-Jews alike. It connects Jews with the Jewishness of the Messiah, and non-Jews with their Jewish roots. Names and key terms are returned to their original Hebrew and presented in easy-to-understand transliterations, enabling the reader to say them the way Yeshua (Jesus) did! 1697 pages.

Hardback	978-9653590151	**JB12**	$34.99
Paperback	978-9653590182	**JB13**	$29.99
Leather Cover	978-9653590199	**JB15**	$59.99
Large Print (12 Pt font)	978-1880226483	**JB16**	$49.99

Also available in French and Portuguese.

Jewish New Testament

—Dr. David H. Stern

The New Testament is a Jewish book, written by Jews, initially for Jews. Its central figure was a Jew. His followers were all Jews; yet no other version really communicates its original, essential Jewishness. Uses neutral terms and Hebrew names. Highlights Jewish references and corrects mistranslations. Freshly translated into English from Greek, this is a must read to learn about first-century faith. 436 pages

Hardback	978-9653590069	**JB02**	$19.99
Paperback	978-9653590038	**JB01**	$14.99
Spanish	978-1936716272	**JB17**	$24.99

Also available in French, German, Polish, Portuguese and Russian.

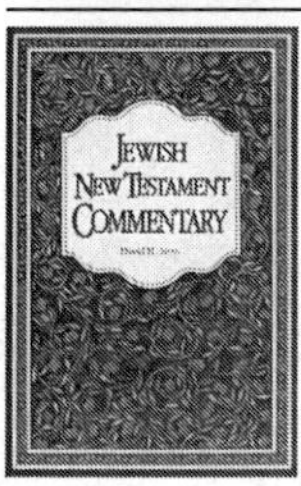

Jewish New Testament Commentary

—Dr. David H. Stern

This companion to the *Jewish New Testament* enhances Bible study. Passages and expressions are explained in their original cultural context. 15 years of research. 960 pages.

Hardback	978-9653590083	**JB06**	$34.99
Paperback	978-9653590113	**JB10**	$29.99

Jewish New Testament on Audio CD or MP3

All the richness of the *Jewish New Testament* beautifully narrated in English by professional narrator/singer, Jonathan Settel. Thrilling to hear, you will enjoy listening to the Hebrew names, expressions and locations as spoken by Messiah.

20 CDs	978-1880226384	**JC01**	$49.99
MP3	978-1880226575	**JC02**	$49.99

Jewish New Testament & Commentary on CD-ROM

Do word searches, studies and more! And, because this is part of the popular LOGOS Bible program, you will have the "engine" to access one of the top Bible research systems. As an option, you'll be able to obtain and cross reference the Mishnah, Josephus, Bible dictionaries, and much more! Windows 3.1+ only.

978-9653590120 **JCD02** $39.99

Messianic Judaism *A Modern Movement With an Ancient Past*

—David H. Stern

An updated discussion of the history, ideology, theology and program for Messianic Judaism. A challenge to both Jews and non-Jews who honor Yeshua to catch the vision of Messianic Judaism. 312 pages

978-1880226339 **LB62** $17.99

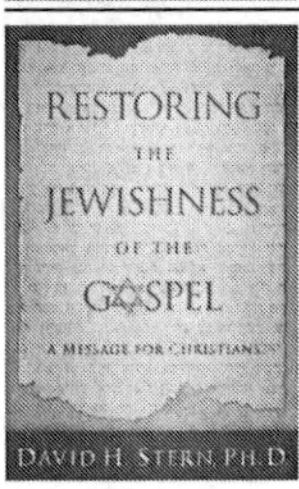

Restoring the Jewishness of the Gospel

A Message for Christians

—David H. Stern

Introduces Christians to the Jewish roots of their faith, challenges some conventional ideas, and raises some neglected questions: How are both the Jews and "the Church" God's people? Is the Law of Moses in force today? Filled with insight! Endorsed by Dr. Darrell L. Bock. 110 pages

English	978-1880226667	**LB70**	$9.99
Spanish	978-9653590175	**JB14**	$9.99

Come and Worship *Ways to Worship from the Hebrew Scriptures*

—Compiled by Barbara D. Malda

We were created to worship. God has graciously given us many ways to express our praise to him. Each way fits a different situation or moment in life, yet all are intended to bring honor and glory to him. When we believe that he is who he says he is [see *His Names are Wonderful!*] and that his Word is true, worship flows naturally from our hearts to his. Softcover, 128 pages.

978-1936716678 LB88 $9.99

His Names Are Wonderful

Getting to Know God Through His Hebrew Names

—Elizabeth L. Vander Meulen and Barbara D. Malda

In Hebrew thought, names did more than identify people; they revealed their nature. God's identity is expressed not in one name, but in many. This book will help readers know God better as they uncover the truths in his Hebrew names. 160 pages.

978-1880226308 **LB58** $9.99

Conveying Our Heritage A Messianic Jewish Guide to Home Practice

—Daniel C. Juster, Th.D. Patricia A. Juster

Throughout history the heritage of faith has been conveyed within the family and the congregation. The first institution in the Bible is the family and only the family can raise children with an adequate appreciation of our faith and heritage. This guide exists to help families learn how to pass on the heritage of spiritual Messianic Jewish life. Softcover, 86 pages

978-1936716739 LB93 $8.99

Mutual Blessing *Discovering the Ultimate Destiny of Creation*

—Daniel C. Juster

To truly love as God loves is to see the wonder and richness of the distinct differences in all of creation and his natural order of interdependence. This is the way to mutual blessing and the discovery of the ultimate destiny of creation. Learn how to become enriched and blessed as you enrich and bless others and all that is around you! Softcover, 135 pages.

978-1936716746 LB94 $9.99

At the Feet of Rabbi Gamaliel

Rabbinic Influence in Paul's Teachings

—David Friedman, Ph.D.

Paul (Shaul) was on the "fast track" to becoming a sage and Sanhedrin judge, describing himself as passionate for the Torah and the traditions of the fathers, typical for an aspiring Pharisee: "…trained at the feet of Gamaliel in every detail of the Torah of our forefathers. I was a zealot for God, as all of you are today" (Acts 22.3, CJB). Did Shaul's teachings reflect Rabbi Gamaliel's instructions? Did Paul continue to value the Torah and Pharisaic tradition? Did Paul create a 'New' Theology? The results of the research within these pages and its conclusion may surprise you. Softcover, 100 pages.

978-1936716753 LB95 $8.99

The Revolt of Rabbi Morris Cohen

Exploring the Passion & Piety of a Modern-day Pharisee

—Anthony Cardinale

A brilliant school psychologist, Rabbi Morris Cohen went on a one-man strike to protest the systematic mislabeling of slow learning pupils as "Learning Disabled" (to extract special education money from the state). His disciplinary hearing, based on the transcript, is a hilarious read! This effusive, garrulous man with an irresistible sense of humor lost his job, but achieved a major historic victory causing the reform of the billion-dollar special education program. Enter into the mind of an eighth-generation Orthodox rabbi to see how he deals spiritually with the loss of everything, even the love of his children. This modern-day Pharisee discovered a trusted friend in the author (a born again believer in Jesus) with whom he could openly struggle over Rabbinic Judaism as well as the concept of Jesus (Yeshua) as Messiah. Softcover, 320 pages.

978-1936716722 LB92 $19.99

Debranding God *Revealing His True Essence*
—Eduardo Stein

The process of 'debranding' God is to remove all the labels and fads that prompt us to understand him as a supplier and ourselves as the most demanding of customers. Changing our perception of God also changes our perception of ourselves. In knowing who we are in relationship to God, we discover his, and our, true essence. Softcover, 252 pages.

978-1936716708 LB91 $16.99

Under the Fig Tree *Messianic Thought Through the Hebrew Calendar*
—Patrick Gabriel Lumbroso

Take a daily devotional journey into the Word of God through the Hebrew Calendar and the Biblical Feasts. Learn deeper meaning of the Scriptures through Hebraic thought. Beautifully written and a source for inspiration to draw closer to Adonai every day. Softcover, 407 pages.

978-1936716760 LB96 $25.99

Under the Vine *Messianic Thought Through the Hebrew Calendar*
—Patrick Gabriel Lumbroso

Journey daily through the Hebrew Calendar and Biblical Feasts into the B'rit Hadashah (New Testament) Scriptures as they are put in their rightful context, bringing Judaism alive in it's full beauty. Messianic faith was the motor and what gave substance to Abraham's new beliefs, hope to Job, trust to Isaac, vision to Jacob, resilience to Joseph, courage to David, wisdom to Solomon, knowledge to Daniel, and divine Messianic authority to Yeshua. Softcover, 412 pages.

978-1936716654 LB87 $25.99

The Return of the Kosher Pig *The Divine Messiah in Jewish Thought*
—Rabbi Tzahi Shapira

The subject of Messiah fills many pages of rabbinic writings. Hidden in those pages is a little known concept that the Messiah has the same authority given to God. Based on the Scriptures and traditional rabbinic writings, this book shows the deity of Yeshua from a new perspective. You will see that the rabbis of old expected the Messiah to be divine. Softcover, 352 pages.

978-1936716456 LB81 $ 39.99

Psalms & Proverbs *Tehillim* תְּהִלִּים-*Mishlei* מִשְׁלֵי
—Translated by Dr. David Stern

Contemplate the power in these words anytime, anywhere: Psalms-*Tehillim* offers uplifting words of praise and gratitude, keeping us focused with the right attitude; Proverbs-*Mishlei* gives us the wisdom for daily living, renewing our minds by leading us to examine our actions, to discern good from evil, and to decide freely to do the good. Makes a wonderful and meaningful gift. Softcover, 224 pages.

978-1936716692 LB90 $9.99

Stories of Yeshua

—Jim Reimann, Illustrator Julia Filipone-Erez

Children's Bible Storybook with four stories about Yeshua (Jesus). *Yeshua is Born: The Bethlehem Story* based on Lk 1:26-35 & 2:1-20; *Yeshua and Nicodemus in Jerusalem* based on Jn 3:1-16; *Yeshua Loves the Little Children of the World* based on Matthew 18:1–6 & 19:13–15; *Yeshua is Alive-The Empty Tomb in Jerusalem* based on Matthew 26:17-56, Jn 19:16-20:18, Lk 24:50-53. Ages 3-7, Softcover, 48 pages.

978-1936716685 LB89 $14.99

Matthew Presents Yeshua, King Messiah *A Messianic Commentary*

—Rabbi Barney Kasdan

Few commentators are able to truly present Yeshua in his Jewish context. Most don't understand his background, his family, even his religion, and consequently really don't understand who he truly is. This commentator is well versed with first-century Jewish practices and thought, as well as the historical and cultural setting of the day, and the 'traditions of the Elders' that Yeshua so often spoke about. Get to know Yeshua, the King, through the writing of another rabbi, Barney Kasdan. 448 pages

978-1936716265 **LB76** $29.99

James the Just Presents Application of Torah

A Messianic Commentary

—Dr. David Friedman

James (Jacob) one of the Epistles written to first century Jewish followers of Yeshua. Dr. David Friedman, a former Professor of the Israel Bible Institute has shed new light for Christians from this very important letter.

978-1936716449 LB82 $14.99

To the Ends of the Earth – How the First Jewish Followers of Yeshua Transformed the Ancient World

— Dr. Jeffrey Seif

Everyone knows that the first followers of Yeshua were Jews, and that Christianity was very Jewish for the first 50 to 100 years. It's a known fact that there were many congregations made up mostly of Jews, although the false perception today is, that in the second century they disappeared. Dr. Seif reveals the truth of what happened to them and how these early Messianic Jews influenced and transformed the behavior of the known world at that time.

978-1936716463 LB83 $17.99

Passion for Israel: *A Short History of the Evangelical Church's Support of Israel and the Jewish People*

—Dan Juster

History reveals a special commitment of Christians to the Jews as God's still elect people, but the terrible atrocities committed against the Jews by so-called Christians have overshadowed the many good deeds that have been performed. This important history needs to be told to help heal the wounds and to inspire more Christians to stand together in support of Israel.

978-1936716401 LB78 $9.99

On The Way to Emmaus: *Searching the Messianic Prophecies*

—Dr. Jacques Doukhan

An outstanding compilation of the most critical Messianic prophecies by a renowned conservative Christian Scholar, drawing on material from the Bible, Rabbinic sources, Dead Sea Scrolls, and more.

978-1936716432 LB80 $14.99

The Red Heifer *A Jewish Cry for Messiah*

—Anthony Cardinale

Award-winning journalist and playwright Anthony Cardinale has traveled extensively in Israel, and recounts here his interviews with Orthodox rabbis, secular Israelis, and Palestinian Arabs about the current search for a red heifer by Jewish radicals wishing to rebuild the Temple and bring the Messiah. These real-life interviews are interwoven within an engaging and dramatic fictional portrayal of the diverse people of Israel and how they would react should that red heifer be found. Readers will find themselves in the Land, where they can hear learned rabbis and ordinary Israelis talking about the red heifer and dealing with all the related issues and the imminent coming and identity of Messiah.

978-1936716470 LB79 $19.99

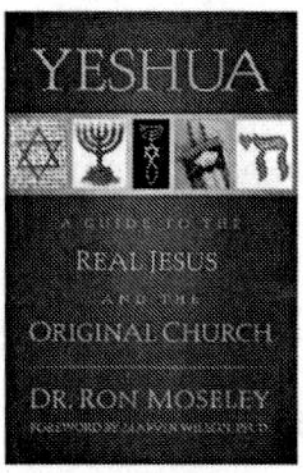

Yeshua *A Guide to the Real Jesus and the Original Church*

—Dr. Ron Moseley

Opens up the history of the Jewish roots of the Christian faith. Illuminates the Jewish background of Yeshua and the Church and never flinches from showing "Jesus was a Jew, who was born, lived, and died, within first century Judaism." Explains idioms in the New Testament. Endorsed by Dr. Brad Young and Dr. Marvin Wilson. 213 pages.

978-1880226681 **LB29** $12.99

The Gospels in their Jewish Context

—John Fischer, Th.D, Ph.D.

An examination of the Jewish background and nature of the Gospels in their contemporary political, cultural and historical settings, emphasizing each gospel's special literary presentation of Yeshua, and highlighting the cultural and religious contexts necessary for understanding each of the gospels. 32 hours of audio/video instruction on MP3-DVD and pdf of syllabus.

978-1936716241 **LCD01** $49.99

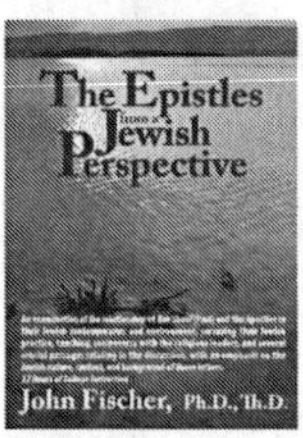

The Epistles from a Jewish Perspective

—John Fischer, Th.D, Ph.D.

An examination of the relationship of Rabbi Shaul (the Apostle Paul) and the Apostles to their Jewish contemporaries and environment; surveys their Jewish practices, teaching, controversy with the religious leaders, and many critical passages, with emphasis on the Jewish nature, content, and background of these letters. 32 hours of audio/video instruction on MP3-DVD and pdf of syllabus.

978-1936716258 **LCD02** $49.99

Gateways to Torah *Joining the Ancient Conversation on the Weekly Portion*

—Rabbi Russell Resnik

From before the days of Messiah until today, Jewish people have read from and discussed a prescribed portion of the Pentateuch each week. Now, a Messianic Jewish Rabbi, Russell Resnik, brings another perspective on the Torah, that of a Messianic Jew. 246 pages.

978-1880226889 **LB42** $15.99

Creation to Completion *A Guide to Life's Journey from the Five Books of Moses*

—Rabbi Russell Resnik

Endorsed by Coach Bill McCartney, Founder of Promise Keepers & Road to Jerusalem: "Paul urged Timothy to study the Scriptures (2 Tim. 3:16), advising him to apply its teachings to all aspects of his life. Since there was no New Testament then, this rabbi/apostle was convinced that his disciple would profit from studying the Torah, the Five Books of Moses, and the Old Testament. Now, Rabbi Resnik has written a warm devotional commentary that will help you understand and apply the Law of Moses to your life in a practical way." 256 pages

978-1880226322 **LB61** $14.99

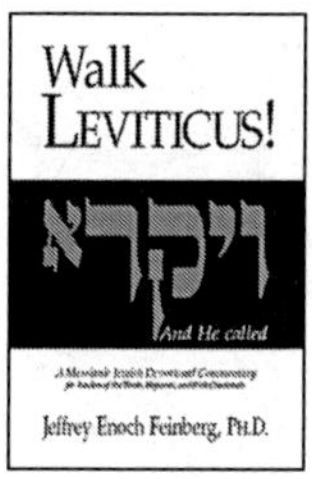

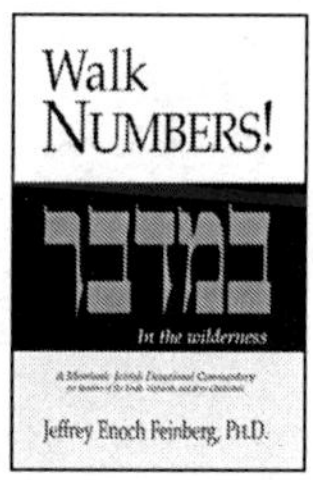

Walk Genesis! Walk Exodus! Walk Leviticus! Walk Numbers! Walk Deuteronomy!

Messianic Jewish Devotional Commentaries

—Jeffrey Enoch Feinberg, Ph.D.

Using the weekly synagogue readings, Dr. Jeffrey Feinberg has put together some very valuable material in his "Walk" series. Each section includes a short Hebrew lesson (for the non-Hebrew speaker), key concepts, an excellent overview of the portion, and some practical applications. Can be used as a daily devotional as well as a Bible study tool.

Walk Genesis!	238 pages	978-1880226759	**LB34**	$12.99
Walk Exodus!	224 pages	978-1880226872	**LB40**	$12.99
Walk Leviticus!	208 pages	978-1880226926	**LB45**	$12.99
Walk Numbers!	211 pages	978-1880226995	**LB48**	$12.99
Walk Deuteronomy!	231 pages	978-1880226186	**LB51**	$12.99
SPECIAL! Five-book Walk!		5 Book Set **Save $10**	**LK28**	$54.99

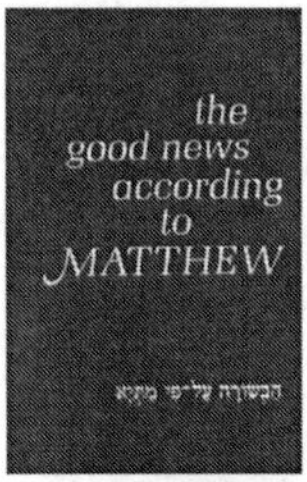

Good News According To Matthew

—Dr. Henry Einspruch

English translation with quotations from the Tanakh (Old Testament) capitalized and printed in Hebrew. Helpful notations are included. Lovely black and white illustrations throughout the book. 86 pages.

978-1880226025 **LB03** $4.99

Also available in Yiddish. **LB02** $4.99

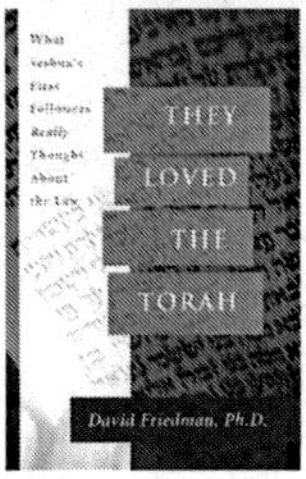

They Loved the Torah *What Yeshua's First Followers Really Thought About the Law*

—Dr. David Friedman

Although many Jews believe that Paul taught against the Law, this book disproves that notion. An excellent case for his premise that all the first followers of the Messiah were not only Torah-observant, but also desired to spread their love for God's entire Word to the gentiles to whom they preached. 144 pages. Endorsed by Dr. David Stern, Ariel Berkowitz, Rabbi Dr. Stuart Dauermann & Dr. John Fischer.

978-1880226940 **LB47** $9.99

The Distortion *2000 Years of Misrepresenting the Relationship Between Jesus the Messiah and the Jewish People*

—Dr. John Fischer & Dr. Patrice Fischer

Did the Jews kill Jesus? Did they really reject him? With the rise of global anti–Semitism, it is important to understand what the Gospels teach about the relationship between Jewish people and their Messiah. 2000 years of distortion have made this difficult. Learn how the distortion began and continues to this day and what you can do to change it. 126 pages. Endorsed by Dr. Ruth Fleischer, Rabbi Russell Resnik, Dr. Daniel C. Juster, Dr. Michael Rydelnik.

978-1880226254 **LB54** $11.99

eBooks Now Available!

All books are available as ebooks for your favorite reader

kindle nook Reader kobo

Visit www.messianicjewish.net for direct links to these readers for each available eBook.

God's Appointed Times *A Practical Guide to Understanding and Celebrating the Biblical Holidays* – **New Edition.**

—Rabbi Barney Kasdan

The Biblical Holy Days teach us about the nature of God and his plan for mankind, and can be a source of God's blessing for all believers–Jews and Gentiles–today. Includes historical background, traditional Jewish observance, New Testament relevance, and prophetic significance, plus music, crafts and holiday recipes. 145 pages.

English	978-1880226353	**LB63**	$12.99
Spanish	978-1880226391	**LB59**	$12.99

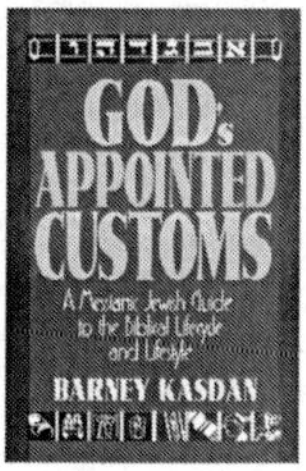

God's Appointed Customs *A Messianic Jewish Guide to the Biblical Lifecycle and Lifestyle*

— Rabbi Barney Kasdan

Explains how biblical customs are often the missing key to unlocking the depths of Scripture. Discusses circumcision, the Jewish wedding, and many more customs mentioned in the New Testament. Companion to *God's Appointed Times*. 170 pages.

English	978-1880226636	**LB26**	$12.99
Spanish	978-1880226551	**LB60**	$12.99

Celebrations of the Bible *A Messianic Children's Curriculum*

Did you know that each Old Testament feast or festival finds its fulfillment in the New? They enrich the lives of people who experience and enjoy them. Our popular curriculum for children is in a brand new, user-friendly format. The lay-flat at binding allows you to easily reproduce handouts and worksheets. Celebrations of the Bible has been used by congregations, Sunday schools, ministries, homeschoolers, and individuals to teach children about the biblical festivals. Each of these holidays are presented for Preschool (2-K), Primary (Grades 1-3), Junior (Grades 4-6), and Children's Worship/Special Services. 208 pages.

978-1880226261 **LB55** $24.99

Passover: *The Key That Unlocks the Book of Revelation*

—Daniel C. Juster, Th.D.

Is there any more enigmatic book of the Bible than Revelation? Controversy concerning its meaning has surrounded it back to the first century. Today, the arguments continue. Yet, Dan Juster has given us the key that unlocks the entire book—the events and circumstances of the Passover/Exodus. By interpreting Revelation through the lens of Exodus, Dan Juster provides a unified overview that helps us read Revelation as it was always meant to be read, as a drama of spiritual conflict, deliverance, and above all, worship. He also shows how this final drama, fulfilled in Messiah, resonates with the Torah and all of God's Word. — Russ Resnik, Executive Director, Union of Messianic Jewish Congregations.

978-1936716210 **LB74** $10.99

The Messianic Passover Haggadah

Revised and Updated

—Rabbi Barry Rubin and Steffi Rubin.

Guides you through the traditional Passover seder dinner, step-by-step. Not only does this observance remind us of our rescue from Egyptian bondage, but, we remember Messiah's last supper, a Passover seder. The theme of redemption is seen throughout the evening. What's so unique about our Haggadah is the focus on Yeshua (Jesus) the Messiah and his teaching, especially on his last night in the upper room. 36 pages.

English	978-1880226292	**LB57**	$4.99
Spanish	978-1880226599	**LBSP01**	$4.99

The Messianic Passover Seder Preparation Guide

Includes recipes, blessings and songs. 19 pages.

English	978-1880226247	**LB10**	$2.99
Spanish	978-1880226728	**LBSP02**	$2.99

The Sabbath *Entering God's Rest*

—Barry Rubin & Steffi Rubin

Even if you've never celebrated Shabbat before, this book will guide you into the rest God has for all who would enter in—Jews and non-Jews. Contains prayers, music, recipes; in short, everything you need to enjoy the Sabbath, even how to observe havdalah, the closing ceremony of the Sabbath. Also discusses the Saturday or Sunday controversy. 48 pages.

978-1880226742 **LB32** $6.99

Havdalah *The Ceremony that Completes the Sabbath*

—Dr. Neal & Jamie Lash

The Sabbath ends with this short, yet equally sweet ceremony called havdalah (separation). This ceremony reminds us to be a light and a sweet fragrance in this world of darkness as we carry the peace, rest, joy and love of the Sabbath into the work week. 28 pages.

978-1880226605 **LB69** $4.99

Dedicate and Celebrate!

A Messianic Jewish Guide to Hanukkah

—Barry Rubin & Family

Hanukkah means "dedication" — a theme of significance for Jews and Christians. Discussing its historical background, its modern-day customs, deep meaning for all of God's people, this little book covers all the how-tos! Recipes, music, and prayers for lighting the menorah, all included! 32 pages.

978-1880226834 **LB36** $4.99

The Conversation

An Intimate Journal of the Emmaus Encounter

—Judy Salisbury

"Then beginning with Moses and with all the prophets, He explained to them the things concerning Himself in all the Scriptures." Luke 24:27
If you've ever wondered what that conversation must have been like, this captivating book takes you there.
"The Conversation brings to life that famous encounter between the two disciples and our Lord Jesus on the road to Emmaus. While it is based in part on an imaginative reconstruction, it is filled with the throbbing pulse of the excitement of the sensational impact that our Lord's resurrection should have on all of our lives." ~ Dr. Walter Kaiser President Emeritus Gordon-Conwell Theological Seminary. Hardcover 120 pages.

Hardcover	978-1936716173	**LB73**	$14.99
Paperback	978-1936716364	**LB77**	$9.99

Growing to Maturity

A Messianic Jewish Discipleship Guide

—Daniel C. Juster, Th.D.

This discipleship series presents first steps of understanding and spiritual practice, tailored for the Jewish believer. It's purpose is to aid the believer in living according to Yeshua's will as a disciple, one who has learned the example of his teacher. The course is structured according to recent advances in individualized educational instruction. Discipleship is serious business and the material is geared for serious study and reflection. Each chapter is divided into short sections followed by study questions. 256 pages.

978-1936716227 **LB75** $19.99

Growing to Maturity Primer: *A Messianic Jewish Discipleship Workbook*

—Daniel C. Juster, Th.D.

A basic book of material in question and answer form. Usable by everyone. 60 pages.

978-0961455507 **TB16** $7.99

Proverbial Wisdom & Common Sense

—Derek Leman

A Messianic Jewish Approach to Today's Issues from the Proverbs Unique in style and scope, this commentary on the book of Proverbs, written in devotional style, is divided into chapters suitable for daily reading. A virtual encyclopedia of practical advice on family, sex, finances, gossip, honesty, love, humility, and discipline. Endorsed by Dr. John Walton, Dr. Jeffrey Feinberg and Rabbi Barney Kasdan. 248 pages.

978-1880226780 **LB35** $14.99

That They May Be One *A Brief Review of Church Restoration Movements and Their Connection to the Jewish People*

—Daniel Juster, Th.D

Something prophetic and momentous is happening. The Church is finally fully grasping its relationship to Israel and the Jewish people. Author describes the restoration movements in Church history and how they connected to Israel and the Jewish people. Each one contributed in some way—some more, some less—toward the ultimate unity between Jews and Gentiles. Predicted in the Old Testament and fulfilled in the New, Juster believes this plan of God finds its full expression in Messianic Judaism. He may be right. See what you think as you read *That They May Be One*. 100 pages.

978-1880226711 **LB71** $9.99

The Greatest Commandment

How the Sh'ma Leads to More Love in Your Life

—Irene Lipson

"What is the greatest commandment?" Yeshua was asked. His reply—"Hear, O Israel, the Lord our God, the Lord is one, and you are to love Adonai your God with all your heart, with all your soul, with all your understanding, and all your strength." A superb book explaining each word so the meaning can be fully grasped and lived. Endorsed by Elliot Klayman, Susan Perlman, & Robert Stearns. 175 pages.

978-1880226360 **LB65** $12.99

Blessing the King of the Universe

Transforming Your Life Through the Practice of Biblical Praise

—Irene Lipson

Insights into the ancient biblical practice of blessing God are offered clearly and practically. With examples from Scripture and Jewish tradition, this book teaches the biblical formula used by men and women of the Bible, including the Messiah; points to new ways and reasons to praise the Lord; and explains more about the Jewish roots of the faith. Endorsed by Rabbi Barney Kasdan, Dr. Mitch Glaser, & Rabbi Dr. Dan Cohn-Sherbok. 144 pages.

978-1880226797 **LB53** $11.99

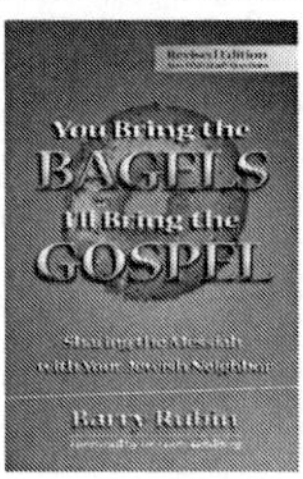

You Bring the Bagels, I'll Bring the Gospel

Sharing the Messiah with Your Jewish Neighbor

Revised Edition—Now with Study Questions

—Rabbi Barry Rubin

This "how-to-witness-to-Jewish-people" book is an orderly presentation of everything you need to share the Messiah with a Jewish friend. Includes Messianic prophecies, Jewish objections to believing, sensitivities in your witness, words to avoid. A "must read" for all who care about the Jewish people. Good for individual or group study. Used in Bible schools. Endorsed by Harold A. Sevener, Dr. Walter C. Kaiser, Dr. Erwin J. Kolb and Dr. Arthur F. Glasser. 253 pages.

English	978-1880226650	**LB13**	$12.99
Te Tengo Buenas Noticias	978-0829724103	**OBSP02**	$14.99

Making Eye Contact With God

A Weekly Devotional for Women

—Terri Gillespie

What kind of eyes do you have? Are they downcast and sad? Are they full of God's joy and passion? See yourself through the eyes of God. Using real life anecdotes, combined with scripture, the author reveals God's heart for women everywhere, as she softly speaks of the ways in which women see God. Endorsed by prominent authors: Dr. Angela Hunt, Wanda Dyson and Kathryn Mackel. 247 pages, hardcover.

978-1880226513 **LB68** $19.99

Divine Reversal

The Transforming Ethics of Jesus

—Rabbi Russell Resnik

In the Old Testament, God often reversed the plans of man. Yeshua's ethics continue this theme. Following his path transforms one's life from within, revealing the source of true happiness, forgiveness, reconciliation, fidelity and love. From the introduction, "As a Jewish teacher, Jesus doesn't separate matters of theology from practice. His teaching is consistently practical, ethical, and applicable to real life, even two thousand years after it was originally given." Endorsed by Jonathan Bernis, Dr. Daniel C. Juster, Dr. Jeffrey L. Seif, and Dr Darrell Bock. 206 pages

978-1880226803 **LB72** $12.99

Praying Like the Jew, Jesus

Recovering the Ancient Roots of New Testament Prayer

—Dr. Timothy P. Jones

This eye-opening book reveals the Jewish background of many of Yeshua's prayers. Historical vignettes "transport" you to the times of Yeshua so you can grasp the full meaning of Messiah's prayers. Unique devotional thoughts and meditations, presented in down-to-earth language, provide inspiration for a more meaningful prayer life and help you draw closer to God. Endorsed by Mark Galli, James W. Goll, Rev. Robert Stearns, James F. Strange, and Dr. John Fischer. 144 pages.

978-1880226285 **LB56** $9.99

Growing Your Olive Tree Marriage *A Guide for Couples from Two Traditions*

—David J. Rudolph

One partner is Jewish; the other is Christian. Do they celebrate Hanukkah, Christmas or both? Do they worship in a church or a synagogue? How will the children be raised? This is the first book from a biblical perspective that addresses the concerns of intermarried couples, offering a godly solution. Includes highlights of interviews with intermarried couples. Endorsed by Walter C. Kaiser, Jr., Rabbi Dan Cohn-Sherbok, Jonathan Settel, Dr. Mitchell Glaser & Natalie Sirota. 224 pages.

978-1880226179 **LB50** $12.99

In Search of the Silver Lining *Where is God in the Midst of Life's Storms?*

—Jerry Gramckow

When faced with suffering, what are your choices? Storms have always raged. And people have either perished in their wake or risen above the tempests, shaping history by their responses...new storms are on the horizon. How will we deal with them? How will we shape history or those who follow us? The answer lies in how we view God in the midst of the storms. Endorsed by Joseph C. Aldrich, Ray Beeson, Dr. Daniel Juster. 176 pages.

978-1880226865 **LB39** $10.99

The Voice of the Lord *Messianic Jewish Daily Devotional*

—Edited by David J. Rudolph

Brings insight into the Jewish Scriptures—both Old and New Testaments. Twenty-two prominent Messianic contributors provide practical ways to apply biblical truth. Start your day with this unique resource. Explanatory notes. Perfect companion to the Complete Jewish Bible (see page 2). Endorsed by Edith Schaeffer, Dr. Arthur F. Glaser, Dr. Michael L. Brown, Mitch Glaser and Moishe Rosen. 416 pages.

9781880226704 **LB31** $19.99

Kingdom Relationships *God's Laws for the Community of Faith*

—Dr. Ron Moseley

Dr. Ron Moseley's Yeshua: A Guide to the Real Jesus and the Original Church has taught thousands of people about the Jewishness of not only Yeshua, but of the first followers of the Messiah.

In this work, Moseley focuses on the teaching of Torah -- the Five Books of Moses -- tapping into truths that greatly help modern-day members of the community of faith.

The first section explains the relationship of both the Jewish people and Christians to the Kingdom of God. The second section lists the laws that are applicable to a non-Jew living in the twenty-first century and outside of the land of Israel.

This book is needed because these little known laws of God's Kingdom were, according to Yeshua, the most salient features of the first-century community of believers. Yeshua even warned that anyone breaking these laws would be least in the Kingdom (Matt. 5:19). Additionally, these laws will be the basis for judgment at the end of every believer's life. 64 pages.

978-1880226841 **LB37** $8.99

Train Up A Child *Successful Parenting For The Next Generation*

—Dr. Daniel L. Switzer

The author, former principal of Ets Chaiyim Messianic Jewish Day School, and father of four, combines solid biblical teaching with Jewish sources on child raising, focusing on the biblical holy days, giving fresh insight into fulfilling the role of parent. 188 pages. Endorsed by Dr. David J. Rudolph, Paul Lieberman, and Dr. David H. Stern.

978-1880226377 **LB64** $12.99

Fire on the Mountain - *Past Renewals, Present Revivals and the Coming Return of Israel*

—Dr. Louis Goldberg

The term "revival" is often used to describe a person or congregation turning to God. Is this something that "just happens," or can it be brought about? Dr. Louis Goldberg, author and former professor of Hebrew and Jewish Studies at Moody Bible Institute, examines real revivals that took place in Bible times and applies them to today. 268 pages.

978-1880226858 **LB38** $15.99

Voices of Messianic Judaism *Confronting Critical Issues Facing a Maturing Movement*

—General Editor Rabbi Dan Cohn-Sherbok

Many of the best minds of the Messianic Jewish movement contributed their thoughts to this collection of 29 substantive articles. Challenging questions are debated: The involvement of Gentiles in Messianic Judaism? How should outreach be accomplished? Liturgy or not? Intermarriage? 256 pages.

978-1880226933 **LB46** $15.99

The Enduring Paradox *Exploratory Essays in Messianic Judaism*

—General Editor Dr. John Fischer

Yeshua and his Jewish followers began a new movement—Messianic Judaism—2,000 years ago. In the 20th century, it was reborn. Now, at the beginning of the 21st century, it is maturing. Twelve essays from top contributors to the theology of this vital movement of God, including: Dr. Walter C. Kaiser, Dr. David H. Stern, and Dr. John Fischer. 196 pages.

978-1880226902 **LB43** $13.99

The World To Come *A Portal to Heaven on Earth*

—Derek Leman

An insightful book, exposing fallacies and false teachings surrounding this extremely important subject... paints a hopeful picture of the future and dispels many non-biblical notions. Intriguing chapters: Magic and Desire, The Vision of the Prophets, Hints of Heaven, Horrors of Hell, The Drama of the Coming Ages. Offers a fresh, but old, perspective on the world to come, as it interacts with the prophets of Israel and the Bible. 110 pages.

978-1880226049 **LB67** .$9.99

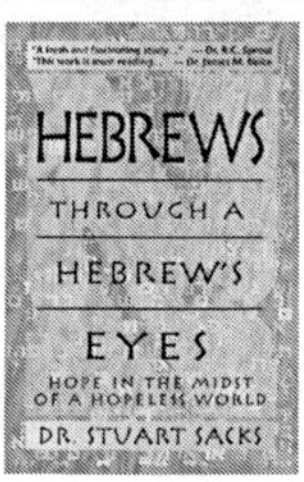

Hebrews Through a Hebrew's Eyes

—Dr. Stuart Sacks

Written to first-century Messianic Jews, this epistle, understood through Jewish eyes, edifies and encourages all. 119 pages. Endorsed by Dr. R.C. Sproul and James M. Boice.

978-1880226612 **LB23** $10.99

The Irrevocable Calling *Israel's Role As A Light To The Nations*

—Daniel C. Juster, Th.D.

Referring to the chosen-ness of the Jewish people, Paul, the Apostle, wrote "For God's free gifts and his calling are irrevocable" (Rom. 11:29). This messenger to the Gentiles understood the unique calling of his people, Israel. So does Dr. Daniel Juster, President of Tikkun Ministries Int'l. In *The Irrevocable Calling*, he expands Paul's words, showing how Israel was uniquely chosen to bless the world and how these blessings can be enjoyed today. Endorsed by Dr. Jack Hayford, Mike Bickle and Don Finto. 64 pages.

978-1880226346 **LB66** $8.99

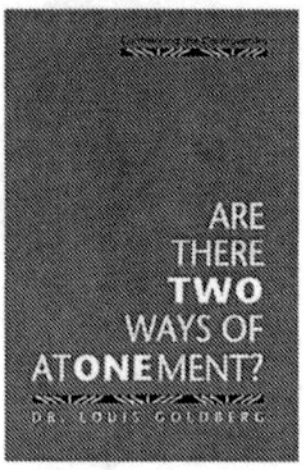

Are There Two Ways of Atonement?

—Dr. Louis Goldberg

Here Dr. Louis Goldberg, long-time professor of Jewish Studies at Moody Bible Institute, exposes the dangerous doctrine of Two-Covenant Theology. 32 pages.

978-1880226056 **LB12** $ 4.99

Awakening *Articles and Stories About Jews and Yeshua*

—Arranged by Anna Portnov

Articles, testimonies, and stories about Jewish people and their relationship with God, Israel, and the Messiah. Includes the effective tract, "The Most Famous Jew of All." One of our best anthologies for witnessing to Jewish people. Let this book witness for you! Russian version also available. 110 pages.

English	978-1880226094	**LB15**	$ 6.99
Russian	978-1880226018	**LB14**	$ 6.99

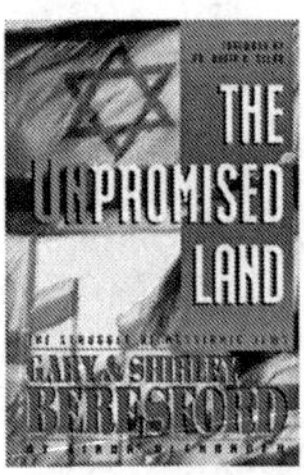

The Unpromised Land *The Struggle of Messianic Jews Gary and Shirley Beresford*

—Linda Alexander

They felt God calling them to live in Israel, the Promised Land. Wanting nothing more than to live quietly and grow old together in the country of refuge for all Jewish people, little did they suspect what events would follow to try their faith. The fight to make *aliyah*, to claim their rightful inheritance in the Promised Land, became a battle waged not only for themselves, but also for Messianic Jews all over the world that wish to return to the Jewish homeland. Here is the true saga of the Beresford`s journey to the land of their forefathers. 216 pages.

978-1880226568 **LB19** $ 9.99

Death of Messiah *Twenty fascinating articles that address a subject of grief, hope, and ultimate triumph.*

—Edited by Kai Kjaer-Hansen

This compilation, written by well-known Jewish believers, addresses the issue of Messiah and offers proof that Yeshua—the true Messiah—not only died, but also was resurrected! 160 pages.

978-1880226582 **LB20** $ 8.99

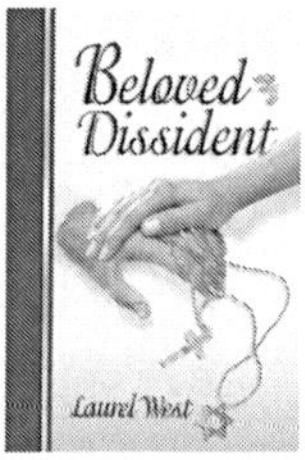

Beloved Dissident *(A Novel)*

—Laurel West

A gripping story of human relationships, passionate love, faith, and spiritual testing. Set in the world of high finance, intrigue, and international terrorism, the lives of David, Jonathan, and Leah intermingle on many levels--especially their relationships with one another and with God. As the two men tangle with each other in a rising whirlwind of excitement and danger, each hopes to win the fight for Leah's love. One of these rivals will move Leah to a level of commitment and love she has never imagined--or dared to dream. Whom will she choose? 256 pages.

978-1880226766 **LB33** $ 9.99

Sudden Terror

—Dr. David Friedman

Exposes the hidden agenda of militant Islam. The author, a former member of the Israel Defense Forces, provides eye-opening information needed in today's dangerous world.

Dr. David Friedman recounts his experiences confronting terrorism; analyzes the biblical roots of the conflict between Israel and Islam; provides an overview of early Islam; demonstrates how the United States and Israel are bound together by a common enemy; and shows how to cope with terrorism and conquer fear. The culmination of many years of research and personal experiences. This expose will prepare you for what's to come! 160 pages.

978-1880226155 **LB49** $ 9.99

It is Good! *Growing Up in a Messianic Family*

—Steffi Rubin

Growing up in a Messianic Jewish family. Meet Tovah! Tovah (Hebrew for "Good") is growing up in a Messianic Jewish home, learning the meaning of God`s special days. Ideal for young children, it teaches the biblical holidays and celebrates faith in Yeshua. 32 pages to read & color.

978-1880226063 **LB11** $ 4.99
